DANGEROUS CROSSING

DANGEROUS CROSSING

Memoir of a fateful trip

C. ROBERT HOLLOWAY

2013

Please Note: Certain names have been changed to honor their privacy.

CONTENTS

A thing is not necessarily true because a man dies for it.
Oscar Wilde—*The Portrait of Mr. WH*

First Call

"I don't think I'm going to make it, C. Bobby. Feels like the top of my head is a cantaloupe and someone is about to take a ball-peen hammer to it. I'm at the end of my rope. I mean it."

"End of your rope, Clive? Ball-peen hammer? And you accuse me of being the hyperbole queen! Not to mention, shameless mixer of metaphors."

"Don't try to deflect my glum with your 'always cheerful no matter how many buckets of crap are thrown your way' speech. In case you haven't heard, Pollyanna died years ago. I only wish she'd taken me with her."

"What an amusing conversation! I can't recall having this much fun since my last root canal."

"You're sounding more like a road company Noel Coward every day. Please, do me a favor? Just shut up and listen. I'm sick of making wine from water, loaves from fishes, or however that Christ thing goes. Borrow from Peter to pay Paul, then Peter wants double interest to compensate for a late payment and tells Paul all the gory details. Then Paul thinks he's been cheated out of being 'made whole'—don't you love that expression? 'Made whole!' Insurance industry lingo. Sounds like something on a scorecard in a whorehouse."

"Scorecard in a whorehouse! Not bad, considering you couldn't possibly know the first thing about it. Look, Ms. Duse, since it was you who called me and asked me to call you back—I'm assuming you're in Malibu?"

"I am, but what difference does that make?"

"Puts it on my dime, so can we please get to the real purpose of your call? Or maybe you don't have one and are determined to work my nerves with your 'misery loves company' sermon?"

"That's mean and unfair. I'm in a terrible place and don't appreciate your insulting me for pouring my heart out to you."

"You're right. I'm sorry. I just now heard the sincerity in your voice. I apologize. So, how can I help—short of lending you money? I just paid off my taxes—I was late again and got hit with severe penalties."

"At least you got them paid. Feels like I'll never get the IRS off my back."

"As you're so fond of saying, "Edit, honey—edit! Cut to the chase. What's really on your mind?"

"I have to go back to New York, C. Bob. Nothing has worked out for me here. I tried real estate; tried reviving my interior design business—painted my ass off—my sister sold a few of my canvases, but not enough to keep me afloat. Then all the writing projects—not even a nibble on any of the screenplays. Nothing, nada. I have to go back to that damned insurance company. I hate the work. I mean the people are mostly nice—there's a couple of throat-cutters…"

"Aren't there always?"

"The job is so boooooring! But I've got to get some income happening. The bosses like me enough to take me back after my 18 month sabbatical…"

"Wow! They let you go on sabbatical for 18 months?"

"I think that's what I called it, at the time."

"So, what do you want from me? I'm struggling to find work, too. You've heard the old adage, 'Win an Academy Award and don't work for two years?' I'm right in the middle of it."

"You didn't *win* it. The movie you *designed* won it."

"All the same. These days the producers are all 24 years old, fresh out of USC or NYU Film School and intimidated by anyone who speaks in complete sentences. So they hire 22 year olds who say, "You know what I'm saying?" before they've said anything. The 24 year olds respond with, "Let me ask you this," and "It's like, it's like…you know what I'm saying?" to an enraptured audience. I come away from interviews feeling older than dirt."

"As Cloris Leachman said to Mary Tyler Moore on the *Rhoda* wedding show, 'Trust me, Mary, that's a very boring story."

"Touché, Clive. And you don't have to preamble that quote every time you use it, since I'm the one who originally called your attention to it. Now, where the hell were we?"

"Oh, that! Well...C. Bobby, I was wondering if you might consider flying out here and sharing the cross-country ride with me. This is my 2nd or 3rd time and I'd rather not go it alone. I'd really appreciate the company. I have a Land Rover—it'll be packed with the two dogs, a couple of my paintings and a shit load of dress suits for the job. We could share the driving. And the cost of gas being what it is..."

"I've driven L.A. to New Orleans two or three times, but I've never driven cross country. How many days does it take, anyway?"

"Some people do it in 5, but I usually take 6 or 7. No sense risking a ticket in Middle America. You saw *Deliverance*. You know what those people are like."

"*Deliverance* was set in the wilds of Georgia. And Burt Reynolds was rafting down a river, as I recall. Other than that, it's the perfect analogy, Clive."

"Are you overdosing on cunt pills, again?"

"Left over from your Christmas gift, remember?"

"So what do you say? Would you do it for me?"

"Might be kind of fun. Can I have a day or two to think on it?"

"When did you start sounding like a grown up? So unlike you." There followed shared nervous laughter.

"I need to make sure the 24 year olds are still determined *not to hire me* and I'll get back to you quick as I can."

"Thanks, C. Bobby. I really need your help, this time. Really, really."

"I hear that and I promise I won't keep you waiting for an answer."

"Thank you. I don't think I could survive one more crossing by myself." The anguish in my friend's voice was unmistakable.

Answering the Call

Clive's plea came at an extremely difficult time for me. I'd recently gone over my limit on two credit cards and was struggling to make minimum payments to keep the banks from downgrading my heretofore stellar credit rating. A prestigious film project came within days of starting pre-production with me as designer, then lost its financing at the last minute. Worse, I'd just learned that my Domestic Partner (West Hollywoodese for 'registered and licensed but not quite married') of 5 ½ years, had dissolved our relationship without informing me and was colluding with the new owners of El Mirador to have me evicted from the rent controlled apartment I'd responsibly maintained for 29 ½ years.

Nevertheless, with the homily, 'When you want something done, find a busy man to do it' reverberating in my head, I used frequent flyer miles to book a one-way flight to Los Angeles and alerted Clive with my decision. He seemed genuinely relieved and assured me I would be handsomely rewarded, if not in this lifetime, over several future ones.

"Spare me the New Age carrots," I chuckled. "That much carotene is bad for both our diets." I flew into LAX on Thursday, picked up a rental car, preceded to El Mirador, where two friends witnessed what appeared to be my lockout, as the key to the master lock refused to be inserted. From there I drove to Kaiser Hospital for an RX pickup and onto the Valley for a haircut, then spent the night at a friend's hillside chalet. Made a gazillion calls Friday related to my impending divorce; met with my new lawyer in Westwood; picked up an RX for Clive at Marvin's in WeHo; visited El Mirador, this time with two friends in tow and discovered the lock had been 'magically' unblocked. Treated the friends to lunch at The French Market as reward for their witness and later viewed a rough cut of the low-budget feature film I'd designed, soon to be released on DVD, despite my assessment that it was a hopeless mish-mash unless augmented with significant reshoots.

I arrived at Clive's Malibu apartment at 6:30 pm. Talked into the night. Saturday, drove back to WeHo and paid final visit to El Mirador

---

with the film's producer as body-guard. Listened to messages on my answering machine, set up remote message retrieval to foil my Ex, returned to Malibu, dined on a yogurt popsicle and drank too many glasses of Trader Joe's Chardonnay, trying to keep apace of Clive's Smirnoffs-on-the-rocks. Collapsed in high-strung exhaustion on his chaise longue/guest pallet at 12:30 am. Slept like a stag surviving hunting season.

Day One

Sunday, May 15th—Malibu, CA to

We were both ruefully hung over that morning. Ignoring our headaches and nausea, we loaded the Rover to the roof, leaving just enough room to place the dog's blankets over a furniture pad, atop stacks of clothing, assorted boxes of household necessities, artist supplies, three of Clive's paintings and his desk-top computer. It was clear the dogs remembered having travelled this way before when they gleefully leaped to the tailgate and wiggled onto their perches.

"Adorable, but how will we be able to see anything through the rear-view mirror," I whined.

"That's what side mirrors are for," Clive snapped. "We haven't left the parking lot and already you're starting with the worries. Not a good sign, C. Bobby. Not a good sign."

"What if we get pulled over? Can't they give you a ticket for having an obstructed view?"

Clive raised his hands to the sky, as if imploring the Gods. "Sweet Jesus, he's a dog with a bone. Would you relax, Mary! We won't get pulled over. And if, by some crazy fluke we do, I'll say the dogs insisted on it. Cops love dogs."

"Okay, but remember, you're the one that brought up *Deliverance.*"

"Yes, Mr. Last Word. And, as you so quickly reminded me, we're not going anywhere near Georgia." He hefted my single piece of luggage, a leather duffle-bag, onto the tailgate. "What in the name of God's teeth do you have in this thing? Your George Foreman grill collection? A rock garden?"

"My humble, single bag is the straw that broke the camel's balls? You said be prepared for six or seven days. Pardon me for wanting clean socks and underwear."

"I didn't say we'd be doing black tie for dinner."

"If there's no room, I'll put the damned thing on skates and rope it to the back of this...Conestoga wagon."

14

"Relax! I'll ask Maggie and Georgie to scoot over and jam it between them. I'm sure they won't mind—just have to take turns breathing, that's all."

"Ah, our first guilt trip of the day. You have to be part Jewish."

Clive flashed his killer smile. "We'll talk about which part, later."

At last, we were ready to leave misty Malibu, but two final tasks awaited us: Clive needed to bid farewell to his 87 year old Mother, who was living in an apartment complex just down the road and I needed to return my rental car to LAX. Los Angeles traffic being what it is, we decided we'd follow each other for both chores.

"Listen, you two," Eva entreated, wagging her finger. I want you to look out for each other on this trip. And drive carefully—there's a lot of crazy people on the roads these days."

"We will," I vowed as I hugged her and climbed back in my car.

"That's got to be an awful long trip, Clive," she fussed. "How many miles is it?"

"Google says 2473," I called out. "As the crow flies."

"Who's Google?" she asked.

"It's a computer thing, Mom," Clive shrugged. "Nothing you'd understand."

"And since we're not crows," I added, "it's more like 28 or 29 hundred miles."

"I made you boys a fresh batch of my empanadillas—from my secret recipe."

"That's wonderful, Mom, but you didn't need to go to all that trouble."

She nodded and shrugged, quite like he'd done. "That's what Mothers do. Here you go—put them in your cooler. There's enough to hold you for a couple of days, if you don't eat 'em all at once."

"Thank you, Mom. Now, we gotta get going." He embraced her for an extended time. "This isn't goodbye, Mom. It's just farewell, for now," he whispered, tears welling in both their eyes.

"I'll miss you every day, my beautiful Son. You've always been my favorite."

"You say that to all your boys, Mom."

"And you always will be…"

"I know, Mom. I know." He held her by her shoulders and looked straight into her blue eyes. "But I gotta get back to New York. Gotta make some money."

"Bob, I want you to remind him to call me every day, you hear? Promise me that?"

"I'll do my best," I shouted as I started my car. "Clive, in case we lose each other, it's Thrifty on Century Blvd—about five blocks west of the Freeway. When you're headed towards the main terminal, you have to make an illegal U-turn to get into the lot."

"I'll be right behind you."

"Bye bye, Eva." I blew her a kiss. "Bye bye, Malibu and helloooooo, Big Apple!" I crooned, to which Eva giggled and Clive rolled his eyes.

As planned, I took surface roads all the way to LAX. Clive stayed close behind me the whole time. My Daytimer indicates it was exactly 10:40 am when I climbed into the passenger seat and called out 'Eastward, Ho!' to which the dogs started barking and my cell phone started ringing. It was Scott, my freshly hired Los Angeles lawyer, calling from his Westwood home (Sunday! Doubletime?), patiently explaining that negotiations with the El Mirador owners weren't going well. Was I prepared to challenge them in a courtroom? Could cost a fortune, given my dual residency. Settling on dates and scheduling witnesses could be very difficult. Luck of the draw could have me pleading before a homophobic, property-owning judge who despised rent control, etc. Finally, Scott needed an additional $3,000. on his retainer as my case was proving more time—consuming than originally estimated. I explained that I was in a friend's SUV, hurtling along the I-10, just passing the LA Convention Center and could he wait until Monday when I could get to a post office in—"Where are we likely to be tomorrow, Clive?"

"Utah."

"…Someplace in Utah."

"I guess that'll be alright," Scott sighed. "To play it safe, better send it special delivery and registered."

"I'll do that. And thanks for your understanding, Scott. Don't hesitate to call with any updates." Suddenly I felt the urge to fudge.

"We're scouting locations for an upcoming road-trip movie. It's a low-budget number, so we're doing it pro bono, on a hand-shake promise I'll get to design it when the producers complete their financing. We'll probably be on the road until next Friday or Saturday."

"Pro bono," Scott verbally winced. "Good luck with that. I'll expect your check no later than Wednesday afternoon, Robert. Safe travels."

"Sounds like a really sympathetic guy," Clive grunted. "Where'd you find him?"

"Gay Yellow Pages or maybe it was somebody at WeHo City Hall. I've forgotten. Picked him after being turned down by two other attorneys. They thought my case sounded too complicated."

"Lawyers! Sometimes I think I was born in the wrong age."

"Speaking of which, you never explained how you got out of the Malibu lease."

"Wasn't aware that I needed to," Clive replied, clearly uncomfortable with the topic.

"Don't get all testy with me. I'm just curious 'cause I know how damned tricky those things can be," I assured him. "How much longer do you have on the lease?"

"Eight or nine months—I can't remember exactly. Anyway, it's all handled. The proximity to Pepperdine helped a lot."

"So you sublet it. Hopefully to one of its professors?"

"No, to a student. Sophomore switching from University of Texas."

"Surprised the building allowed it. They're usually so damned finicky about subletting. What did you tell them?"

"Jesus, Jessica Fletcher! Do you have to know everything?"

"Yes, I do. How else can I keep the streets of Cabot Cove safe?"

"I told the managers a little fib—that he was a relative—my nephew, to be exact."

"Ah, the age-old 'Nephew' ruse. Has a reassuring ring to it, despite freighting a whiff of homo-eroticism."

"Finally found a way to use 'freighting' in a sentence, did you? But doesn't 'freighting a whiff' strike you as overkill?"

"You missed your calling, Clive. Should have been an English professor—and get paid to correct anyone and everybody for the slightest infraction."

"Don't think I haven't given it some thought."

"So what's this kid like? Smart? Cute? Eager? Scholarly?"

"The latter and very shy. His Father—obviously very protective—flew in from Austin to *interview me*. Nice man—we talked at length. The boy's name is Oliver—but the Father did most of the talking."

"And he was okay with the 'nephew' story?"

"He warmed up to it after I told him some of my reasons for returning to New York. Thank God, he didn't ask me for a birth-to-death accounting, *like certain people I know*."

"I hope you got a couple months in advance? And some kind of security deposit?"

"I did and that's also none of your business."

"So Oliver or his Dad mails you a check and you pay your landlords?"

"Yes and yes. It's how I could afford the deposit and lease on the New York apartment." Clive seemed agitated, bordering on morose.

"Thanks for filling me in. You know I'll help if I can."

"Okay, but you know I hate talking about financial crap. Always have—always will. Fast as I get some money coming in, I can begin to get caught up. Now, can we be done with it?"

"Your wish, my command." I decided to switch topics by asking one of his favorite riddles. "So tell me, darling, how does Sylvia look, now that she's thin?"

"Fat!" he spat out, relieving the tension and sending us into gales of laughter.

"Time for a coffin nail. Always cheers me up." With that, he lit up.

"Please Clive, if you're going to smoke, either roll down your window or pull over and park. I'm getting nauseous. Another minute and I'll be throwing up."

"Drama Queen! You were a bigger smoker than I ever was. Three or four packs a day, I recall. I find it hard to believe a little second-hand smoke is going to make you throw up."

"Well, it will. And I'd rather not prove it. First hand, second hand—it's all the same. Please roll down your window so we can enjoy the 70 mile an hour cyclone whipping around us."

He placed the cigarette in his mouth at a defiant angle and lowered his window. "There, will that shut you up, Holloway?" he shouted over the din."

"Like being inside a NASA test tunnel. Always a thrill."

He glanced into the rear-view mirror. "Maggie and Georgie are loving it."

"I can't believe, after all the deaths from lung cancer you've witnessed, you're still smoking!" I yelled.

"Spare me! An occasional puff isn't going to kill me nearly as fast as having to deal with all the other crappy issues in my life." He inhaled deeply, defiantly. "Calms my nerves—simple as that."

"Calms yours and works mine. Besides making me nauseous, it gives me a migraine and I don't normally get migraines." He took two more quick puffs, carefully tamped it out in the ashtray, placed the butt in his shirt pocket and rolled the window up.

"Thank you. I hope to regain my hearing in a few minutes."

"And wipe the acid from your tongue, while you're at it."

"I thought you'd quit for good—a couple years back. Underwent hypnosis at UCLA. You said it worked."

"I did and it did—for a few months, but eventually the spell wore off and one thing led to another…"

"Jesus! Look what they cost these days. What is it—$5.00 a pack?"

"Even more in a machine," he allowed.

"When I lived in St. Thomas, cigarettes were $2.00 a *carton*. That was my excuse for smoking so much. Thank God, I quit. I'd be spending $20. a day, now."

"They say you reformed smokers are like reformed whores. Holier than thou—sanctimony redefined."

"Did it cold turkey. Only thing that worked for me. And it lasted. Despite the awful side-effects during the first month, if you can get through it—it lasts."

"And made you fat. You showed me pictures—you looked like the Michelin Tire Boy—with a tan."

"How kind of you to remember. Afterwards, I did one of those 30 day water fasts and dropped 29 pounds."

"29 pounds in 30 days. And you're on my ass about what's unhealthy? Give me a break!"

"True, I paid for it with the heart-attack twenty years later. But that's all blood under the bridge, as you like to say."

"Tell the truth. You must have a craving, once in a while. Yearn for a warm puff on a cold day."

"I did, for the first year or so. Went to smoky bars just to see what it was like. Test my resolve. Wasn't long before I was hating it— always coughing up phlegm the next morning. All these years later, being around smokers still produces the same hideous effect."

"So, what do you suggest we do for the next six days?"

"Let's strike a deal. When you need to smoke, we'll take a break and pull over. If you can time your nicotine fixes to when the dogs need to do their duty, more the better."

"Fixes! You make it sound like I'm shooting up."

"Well, it *is* an addiction, My Liege."

"You'd have me wearing a Scarlet A."

"No. The trade off is us pulling over and you smoking outside the van."

"Great. Shouldn't add more than a day or two to our trip," he laughed. "God help me, I'm sounding like you."

"If it gets you to cut back on the cancer sticks, how bad can that be?"

"I'll try to hold that thought the next time I cross the country— *alone*."

"Isn't it rich? Aren't we a pair?" I began to sing. "Me here at last on the ground…"

He joined in. "You in mid-air. Send in the clowns."

I gestured for him to solo in his flawless tenor. "Isn't it rich? Isn't it queer, Losing my timing this late in my career?"

Noticing a slight catch in his voice, I jumped in. "And where are the clowns? There ought to be clowns."

We sang the last line in make-shift harmony, which surprised us both for sounding pretty good. "Well, maybe next year." I reached over and squeezed his hand.

"Good," he allowed. "That was good. Still, I think you'd better keep your day job, C. Bobby."

It was Clive's intention that, by the end of the first day, we would reach Cisco, Utah, the ghost town close to the Colorado border, not factoring in the stresses the previous night's indulgences and the packing and farewells had fostered. By 11:45, despite wolfing down two each of Eva's spicy pies, we were famished and pulled into a TGIF at Covina, CA, enticed by a banner heralding its '$9.99 Family Brunch Special.' Thus began a succession of fast and cheap, forgettable meals at thrice daily stops to let Maggie and Georgie relieve themselves while we refueled the gas guzzling Land Rover at $60. to $80. a pump.

After brunch, I took my first stint at the wheel and set cruise control at precisely 65 miles per hour. Since we were on the long stretch of unbending highway leading to Las Vegas, Clive thought I was being needlessly cautious.

"You can push it to 75, Miss Priss. Look at that line of cars behind us. They're giving us the finger every time they pass."

"Did I make critical comments when you were driving?"

"I don't recall," he smirked.

"Let me help you. I didn't. So please return the courtesy."

A few minutes later, as we descended the first big hill, we glimpsed the whirling lights of two Sheriff's vehicles. They'd pulled over two of the pick-ups that had flashed their fingers and careened around us. Unable to restrain myself, I observed haughtily, "CHP's version of *Deliverance*, perhaps?"

"God's teeth!" Clive cursed. "Am I going to hear about that for the next 3000 miles?"

"Not if we stick to the speed limit. Maybe an eencie 2 or 3 miles over it."

"Without sounding like I'm about to beat a dead horse...," I said.

"Which usually means that's exactly what you're getting ready to do," Clive interjected.

"You're right. But, if you can forgive the Old West metaphor, I have to say I'll never understand why you didn't become a major star."

"Not *that* dead horse, again." He shook his head. "You sound like my Mother."

"God knows, you had all the qualifications—singer-dancer-actor—talent in spades—looks to die for. I used to tell everyone, I never had to worry about crossing the street when I was with you. One glance at you and traffic came to a screeching halt. Made for a safe crossing every time."

"Nobody can ever take away your Hyperbole Queen crown, C. Bob."

"That's comforting, but what do you think happened, Clive? What got in the way? I figure something awful must have taken place, somewhere along the line?"

"Some *things*, is more like it. But what's the point in talking about it at this late date?"

"What better time? We've got the next six or seven days to keep each other awake and alert."

"My story is so clichéd—nothing you haven't heard before."

"Nevertheless, inquisitive friends and inquiring fans want to hear it from the horse's mouth."

"For one thing, I hated feeling like a pawn in the Hollywood casting game—always at the whim of so many assholes," Clive shrugged. "I hated it even more than Tom did."

"Unless you padded your resume, it shows you had considerable success, from the get go. Movies, TV guest shots—a soap opera..."

"That's all true. What it doesn't show is all the humiliating, degrading, crappy stuff that took place between jobs."

"If you're referring to rejection, doesn't that go with the territory? Isn't rejection an actor's middle name?"

"You've been watching too much Dr. Phil. They've raised rejection to a Machiavellian art form in Hollywood. Case in point: after several readings and screen tests, I was cast by Ivan Tors as the second lead opposite Chuck Connors in a TV series called *Cowboy in Africa*, set on a game preserve in Kenya. In the story, Connors was hired by the owner to introduce modern methods to his game ranch. He brings along his helper and best friend, a Navajo Indian named John Henry—that was going to be me."

"I could see you in braids and feathers."

"You won't after you hear this story." Clive sighed and took a deep breath. "When I was hired two weeks earlier, I was told to let my hair grow and work on my tan. Obedient soldier that I was, I did everything they told me and reported to the Columbia Ranch, early on a Monday morning—the first day of filming. Right away, I sensed something wasn't right when Wally, the guard at the gate, greeted me in a weird tone. When I got to the make-up trailer, I was met by an AD who said I shouldn't bother to go inside. I'd been replaced."

"Wow! And nobody bothered to call you over the weekend? Where was your agent?"

"I was too upset to ask. Tors was known as a cut-throat SOB—incapable of feeling embarrassment, so nobody thought it was a question of him being too embarrassed to call Dick."

"What about your contract?"

"Hadn't been given one yet. That was SOP in series television—still is. Contracts get signed weeks, often months after a show has been filmed."

"So what happened?"

"I was in such shock, I don't even remember driving home."

"I can only imagine…"

"No, you can't. Nobody can, really. Couldn't have come at a worse time—I'd left the soap opera to take the series. Tom and I were already banking on the income."

"Anybody ever give a reason for your replacement?"

"Sometime later, Dick learned that Chuck Conners was worried about my being too pretty—'too light in the loafers' to quote him exactly."

"I recall hearing rumors that Connors had a yen for pretty boys himself."

"That was the scuttlebutt, but as I said then and I'll say it now—he could die with the secret, as far as I was concerned."

"And he did. Back in the early 90's, I think."

"Eventually, when we got over our shock, Tom and I referred to that scenario as 'A Star is Stillborn.' Does that answer your question?"

"As the actress said to the Bishop, 'Jesus Christ, what a business!"

At 4:30 we crossed the California/Nevada border—admitted we were exhausted and decided Las Vegas was as far as we could make it.

"Motel Sixes are one of the few chains that allow dogs," Clive announced. "Call information and find the closest one. If I remember correctly, it's on the East side of Downtown."

"Information on a cell phone costs a fortune."

"Here, use mine," he hissed, barely containing his anger. "I'm switching servers soon as we get to New York, anyway."

After three tries and twice losing the signal, I was connected (for an additional fee of $2.00) to the Motel 6 on Boulder Highway. On assuring the manager that the dogs were somewhat smaller than Brahma bulls, he offered us a double for $39. plus tax.

Source: www.motel6.com

Motel 6 Las Vegas Boulder Highway
4125 Boulder Hwy, Las Vegas, NV 89121
(702) 457-8051 (800) 466-8356 (702) 457-0265 (Fax)
This Motel 6 is located 6 miles from the Strip & downtown Las Vegas. Amenities include: Coin Laundry, Outdoor Pool, Public Transportation & Restaurant Nearby.

It had been a long time since I'd stayed in a Motel 6, so I wasn't prepared for the brutal assault on my olfactory senses. Walking past the pool, the burning scent of chlorine set the dogs to whining and bleached the cuffs on my chinos. Entering the room, we were blinded by the neon-blue paisley spreads, then brought to blinking resuscitation by the antiseptically reassuring ammonia fumes.

"I'll put Maggie and Georgie back in the Rover," Clive declared. "Turn the A/C on full blast and leave the front door open for a few minutes. That ought to do the trick."

"And if it doesn't, can we check into a Days Inn or maybe "The Bates Motel?" I pleaded.

"Get over yourself. Can't all be the Ritz. Especially when you're travelling with pets."

"Feels like the hairs are gone from my nostrils."

"They were too long, anyway. Stay here and guard the fort. I'll run to the store and find us some supper. You like KFC and I'm running low on Smirnoff's."

"KFC is fine. I'm so hungry, I'm ready to eat my shoes, if they hadn't been so badly…"

"…Bleached," Clive said in chorus. "I hope this isn't a preview of tomorrow's dissertation?"

"It will be if these fumes don't dissipate. I'll call it my 'Dissipation Dissertation."

Clive giggled, "Could you squeeze any more 'esses' in there?" With that, he tapped my shoulder and disappeared for half an hour.

It was approaching 9:30 when we polished off the Colonel's original recipe breasts and legs, Cole slaw, corn on the cob and oddly sweet biscuits. For dessert, I bought a packet of Oreo's from the machine in the lobby and Clive poured his fourth and final vodka.

With the ammonia smell mostly gone and numbed by Napa grapes and Ukrainian potatoes, we hit our separate sacks, vowing to shower in the morning. The dogs curled up on his while I determined not to snore too loudly on mine.

"I should warn you," Clive mumbled. "Maggie's a snorer. I do what I can to keep her quiet, but I can't guarantee it."

"I'm told I am too, but I sleep on my stomach, which seems to minimize the thunder."

"Don't worry. I'll shake you if it gets too bad."

"Last two nights in Malibu—you were cutting some serious Zs, yourself, my Prince. Made Maggie sound like *Johnny Belinda*."

"Johnny Belinda!" he snorted. "You pulled that one out your ass—sorry—past. I *do not* snore."

"Wish I'd brought my tape recorder."

"Well, you didn't, Blanche. You didn't. Now shut up and go to sleep."

"One more thing: You know how I love to play the title game?"

"Does he ever give it a rest?" Clive moaned.

"Almost as much as you like to play the casting game. Anyway, I thought of a title for our trip. Want to hear it?"

"If you promise it's the last thing coming out of your mouth."

"Since we're crossing America the wrong way round, I think we should call it, *The Reverse Mormon Conquest*."

"Jesus, Holloway! For that, you kept me awake?"

"It's okay. I have an alternate. How's *How The East Was Won*?"

"Georgie, you have my permission to bite him—hard. Start on his mouth."

"Love you, Clive."

"I used to love you."

"It'll come back. Goodnight, Sweet Prince."

"Goodnight, Gracie! Where's the duct tape when you need it?"

Day Two

Monday, May 16th—Las Vegas to

As is my pattern when overly anxious, I awoke at dawn, showered as quietly as I could, given the confines of the room, and at 6:30, went outside to call my Mother in New Jersey, presuming the three hour time difference would have her long up and well into her day. "Hi, Mother, it's your son."

"I was just on my way over to the Acme."

"Want me to call back later?"

"No. It can wait. Where in the world are you, Bobby? I called your Los Angeles number I don't know how many times yesterday. At least I think it was your Los Angeles number—you have so darn many of them."

"Just two these days. Home and cellphone."

"Didn't you get my message? I left it on that answer thing."

"No, I didn't. I'm sorry, Mother. I was staying out in Malibu. I thought I told you I was helping Clive get ready to drive across country."

"If you did, I don't remember. Who's Clive?"

"Mother, you've met him several times. Harry and you had supper with him over at the beach a couple of summers ago—when he directed "A Chorus Line" at The Surflight."

"Oh, that guy. Very nice, very polite—good lookin' too, as I remember. Harry and me, we both loved that show, but I remember you spent a fortune on those tickets. Way too much. So where are you now?"

"Las Vegas. We're about to leave…"

"Las Vegas! What in the world for? You got money to throw away?"

"No, Mother. We're not here to gamble. Haven't been near a casino, nor are we likely to. Like I said, we're driving across country. Just happened to land here after our first day on the road. Clive has a job waiting for him in New York City. He asked me to come along. Wanted company and somebody to share the driving."

"That so? Is he doing another Broadway show? Maybe he can get you a job with it?"

"Afraid not, Mother. He's going back to work for an insurance company. They insure apartment buildings and private residences—all over Manhattan. Big business since 9/11."

"I'm sure he'd rather be doing something else but at least it'll bring in some steady money. These are tough times, I don't have to tell you."

"How well I know."

"Maybe it's time you started thinkin' about gettin' into some other kind of business, Bobby? You must be gettin' awful tired of that 'feast and famine' stuff by now?"

"Mother, let's not go down that road again, please? Besides, what am I going to do—be a greeter at WalMart? A night manager at McDonald's?"

"Don't be a Smart Alec. There's nothing the matter with good, honest work, Bobby. You remember your cousin Skipper down in Florida? The one owned his own airplane? You heard he committed suicide?"

"You've told me several times, Mother."

"Upped and killed himself. Lost a contract with some big company, couldn't see any other way out."

"I'm sorry to hear that, Mother. I really am, but…"

"Broke his family's heart—all over money." A telling silence followed.

"Again, I'm sorry, Mother, but I hold on to the idea that by thinking positively and promoting, promoting, promoting, something will come along. It always has."

"You're getting' on, you know? You're not a kid anymore. How old are you, anyway? I forget."

"You were 20 when you had me. Do the math."

"To do that, I'd have to remember how old I am," she laughed. "I'll figure it out later. Now I'm late for the Acme. Out of practically everything—lunch meat, bread, waffles, those oatmeal cookies Harry likes. I like to get there before the crowds."

"I understand, Mother. I'll call you after we get to New York."

"I certainly hope so, and bein' that close, would it kill you to come see me?"

"No, but you just erased any element of surprise."

"Just show up—I'll looked surprised," to which we both hooted.

"I love you, Mother."

"Love you too, Bobby. Now drive carefully. There's a lot of crazy people on the road, these days."

I started to say, "That must be generic dialogue for Mothers," but she'd already hung up. I was feeling weirdly out of sorts about our conversation, wondering why, after all these years, I never had the temerity to lay the whole, unvarnished truth on her. Here I was, losing my beautiful apartment of 30 years, my 'domestic partner' threatening to haul me into court for totally irreprehensible cause, costing me thousands in legal fees, not to mention my cherished tranquility and joy in dual residency—all of it about to reduce my Los Angeles life to rubble. Yet, I was still putting a shine on my situation to Mother, if not by sugar-coating it, by flat out omission. For the thousandth time, I asked myself, 'When will I feel confident enough to tell Mother exactly like it is?' For the thousandth and one time, I answered, 'After she's gone seems about right.'

I stopped by the lobby and filled two Styrofoam cups with complimentary coffee. Clive was toweling off after his shower when I stepped into the room.

"Slept like the dead," he declared. "How about you?"

"Me too. If anyone was snoring, I didn't hear it." I placed his cup on the sink. "I brought you this, which the sign at the front desk says is coffee, but I think somebody is lying."

"I'm not a coffee drinker," he reminded. "Hate the taste and I'd be peeing every half hour if I drank it. Goes right through me."

"I have to eat a decent breakfast or I get a headache and end up chewing on my elbow."

"There's a picture! It's yogurt and tea for me."

"I saw a McDonald's commercial recently where it said they've added a fruit and yogurt bowl to their breakfast menu."

"I'll believe that when I see it," he sniffed as he hitched the dog's leashes. "Would you put our bags in the Rover while I walk the ladies?"

"Sure. Then can we look for a McDonald's? Love their Big Breakfast. Gets my recommend daily ration of styrofoam, crammed into one meal."

"Think I saw one in the next block—if you insist."

"Great. While you're walking the dogs, I'll use the toilet. Feeling the Colonel's wrath."

"Thanks for sharing," he snickered. "Gives new meaning to *What happens in Vegas, stays in Vegas.*"

"Well done," I guffawed. "Joan Rivers' everything will sag in envy when she hears that one."

We handed in our room keys, made sure there were no hidden charges and drove to the nearby McDonald's, which, miraculously, was offering their new yogurt and fruit breakfast for under $3.00 so I decided to do the healthy thing, as well.

Shortly after leaving Las Vegas, we entered territory I'd never seen before. I kept busy looking for photo-op landmarks and eventually spotted a wriggling family of snakes preparing to cross the highway.

"Slow down, Clive. Looks like a bunch of rattlesnakes just ahead."

"There's no such thing as a 'bunch' of snakes. A group of snakes is called a rhumba."

"Like the dance? You can't be serious?"

"But it's spelled with an 'h' and pronounced exactly like the dance," he intoned.

"Seems totally bizarre…"

"I know it's right 'cause Tom toyed with using 'rhumba' in "Crowned Heads"—in that scene with Lorna and the snakes in Mexico. After an extended argument—you know how he loved exotic words—I convinced him not to. Afraid it might provoke a laugh at a crucial moment. Eventually, he thanked me."

"Well, I'll be hornswoggled, Pardner. Lairnin' somethin' new ever' day." Unable to leave it alone, I teased, "So, if we see a bunch of turtles, do we call them a Tarantella?"

"No, but if you spot another rhumba of rattlers, I'll pull over and offer them a new dance partner."

"Another zinger, and we're nowhere near Salt Lake City, that fountainhead of Stand-up."

"Nor are we going to stop there. Got to make up for yesterday. I'd like to make it to someplace in Colorado—like Vail."

"Whatever you say. You're the one who's done this before. Don't forget I have to find a post office and mail that check to my lawyer."

Clive shook his head. "What an ungrateful little shit that Ronnie turned out to be—after all you did for him. And evil! That man is evil!"

"Most every one of my friends urged me to dump him years ago— but I kept thinking if I hung in and wasn't too judgmental or authoritarian, I could make things go right. I also thought it was good exercise for me—a way to work on compromise and try to bridge the generation gap."

"And play rescuer. Admit it C. Bobby. You're Florence Nightingale disguised as a self-centered queen."

"What a sweet compliment. I must remember to repeat it to Mother. It'll make her so proud."

"Don't get all bent out of shape. You know it's true."

"Etymology comes into play here. I prefer to think of myself as a 'fuser' rather than a rescuer. You, on the other hand, might be categorized as a 'resistor' in that you don't fuse with new acquaintances easily."

"Is this a rehearsal for your appearance on 'Oprah?'"

"Not unless you're planning on a detour to Chicago," I countered. "What's the matter, Clive? Can't handle it when the other shoe fits?"

"Your metaphorical riffs become more unintelligible by the hour."

"Maybe it's time to turn on the radio?" So I did, starting with the FM stations which had the franchise on Country, Christian Contemporary and the Top-40. Clive said he could handle Country and maybe a bit of Top-40, but neither of us could endure more than a few minutes of Christian Contemporary (big orchestra, lush arrangements, insipid lyrics, cloyingly sung) so I switched to AM which offered non-stop Rush Limbaugh and Doctor Laura—both impossible to digest, even after our wholesome McDonald's breakfast.

"Turn it off," he commanded and we drove on in a few minutes of silence. "What kind of people listen to that man, anyway? He's scary."

"My brother-in-law, for one," I said. "Listens to him religiously. Dominick is a great husband and father, great provider—generous to a fault—reasonably sane on many subjects. But he's a hard Right-Winger—intransigent Republican. Dom thinks the sun rises and sets on Limbaugh and his ilk."

"Like my sister," he responded. She's become more and more conservative over the years. I figure it's to please her man who sounds a lot like your brother-in-law. Still, Bret's been great to her. Worships the ground she walks on."

"As Dominick does with my sister," I said, just as a sign indicating we were approaching the Arizona border caught my eye. "Have we made a wrong turn? What the heck are we doing in Arizona? I thought Utah was next over from Nevada?"

"Look at the map, Mr. Eagle Scout. We pass through the north western tip of Arizona for about 35 miles. Gotta' look fast, or you'll miss it."

"Ah, you're right. Who knew?" I smiled, delighted at learning a new geographical tidbit.

"If only the terrain was half as interesting as the map," Clive mused.

"So how do you handle it when you're with them?"

"Don't talk politics—ever. Makes for some convoluted conversations, but I try never to trigger an upset. Not worth it."

"Agreed. And I have to avoid religion as well. They're devout Catholics and find no humor whatsoever in jokes about priests or nuns. So I save my best punchlines for my cloth-wearing friends."

"Very sly. 'And exactly how many of them are there?' Oprah asks."

"Jokes or priests and nuns?"

"Enough already. I feel like we're in a Sit-com and it's about to be cancelled."

"Shall I turn on the radio again?"

"Spare me," he huffed.

"Okay. How about if I shut up completely?"

"Not your style. And, besides, that would defeat the main reason for your being here, wouldn't it?"

"Thank you for your noblesse oblige, Your Highness. I'd like to think of myself as your humble servant and snappy Court Jester—at least for the duration of this trip."

"Snappy I could see, but 'humble'—no way. It's the last word I'd ever use to describe you, C. Robert Holloway."

"As you wish, Your Majesty. Changing gears, I just thought of a long-overdue 'Thank You' I owe you."

"If this is some kind of trick, I don't want to hear it."

"No trick. It's real. My Mother and Daddy never forgot that evening when you had them for cocktails at your house up on Hedges Way. They'd never seen anything so glamorous or dramatic. Afterwards, Mother said, 'That house was like something from the movies.'"

"Only for you did I do it. Never been comfortable entertaining other people's parents."

"Thank you for breaking your rules. My Dad thought your mirrored fireplace was the coolest thing he'd ever seen and how neat it was to see the sunset over Los Angeles reflected in it. Daddy, being a pragmatist, wondered if the heat from the fire had ever broken the glass."

Clive chuckled. "No, it was insulated all around the opening so the heat couldn't hurt it, but my floor-man did when he lost control of his buffer and the thing rammed one of the side panels. Cracked it so bad, the whole mirror had to be replaced, floor to ceiling. Cost a fortune."

"Wouldn't your earthquake insurance cover it?"

"Tried that, but since there hadn't been an earthquake in LA for a couple of years, my State Farm agent thought it might be a tough sell."

"Honesty is always the best policy," I pontificated.

"Remind me to write that down," he smiled, as he slipped into low gear to accommodate the steep incline just ahead.

"Not to belabor the point," I continued, "but may I also remind you that I entertained your family at a sit-down dinner at El Mirador, some time before you hosted mine?

"Remind me all you want," Clive grumbled with a grin, "doesn't mean I have to remember it."

"I remember slaving over a gourmet meal of Caesar's salad, wild rice and broiled salmon, only to learn at the last minute that your step-Dad wouldn't touch salmon."

"That sounds right."

"I think I slathered a chicken breast with garlic butter and tossed it in the microwave, at the last minute."

"Anything with butter would have made James happy. Not so sure about the garlic."

"Your Mother and sister thought it was all wonderful and wrote me a sweet note afterwards."

"As your Mother did to me," Clive confirmed. "Obviously we both come from bloodlines with good manners."

"Makes you wonder what went wrong with us," I pondered in pseudo-angst.

"What's to wonder?" he snapped. "You're a selfish C-Word and I'm a saint waiting to be canonized."

It was approaching 1:00 pm when we arrived at Beaver, Utah and pulled into the post office on Main Street. The clerk greeted me with that cautious smile small-town folks reserve for the stranger-with-the-funny-accent, then coached me through the forms for a registered, special delivery letter. I thanked him and asked if he knew of a good place to have lunch nearby. He said we were a little late, but if we hurried, Maria's Cocina was about a mile away, in the campgrounds on the hillside, just off the main highway. "Plenty locals go there, so it must be good."

I couldn't resist. "You ever go there?"

He flushed slightly. "Si, Senor. It's my Auntie's place. Everything is homemade. I help her out sometimes—de noche."

"I'll tell her you sent us, Xavier—assuming your aunt's name is Maria?"

"Si, si, but she won't be there this late. Her son will. My cousin. His name's Fernando."

"Muchas gracias, Xavier."

Clive wasn't too happy about having to drive so far off the main highway—but Maria's Cocina, huddled under giant fir trees, with a huge oven dominating the rustic dining area, proved to be a real find.

"Since you'll be driving after lunch," Clive declared, "I just might have a cerveza or two."

As touted by her nephew, everything was home-made at Maria's—guacamole had a secret kick, tortillas were meaty and flavorful. By the end of the meal, we were considerably energized and tipped Fernando accordingly. As we left the restaurant and walked toward the Rover, the dogs commenced to squeal in delight at the sight of their handsome master. Clive handed me the keys—I turned the ignition and checked the gas gauge which registered just over ½ tank. "Lookin' good. Enough to get us another half mile, or so."

"Very funny. You can relax—it's my turn at the next pump," Clive winked. "Now fasten your seat belt and drive this chariot the hell out of Beaver or Snatch or whatever this God forsaken place is called." After I'd steered us back onto the highway, he resumed, deadpan. "You know, I still have mixed emotions."

"How's that?" I asked, not anticipating his answer.

"Over you introducing me to Scientology."

"Jesus, Clive! How many more years have to pass before you quit beating that dead horse?"

"Maybe twenty," he grinned.

Hoping to deflect any further discussion on the subject, I turned on the radio, but still couldn't find anything but more Rush and Evangelical rantings.

"Scientology was a mixed blessing at best," Clive mused.

"And a criminal cult at worst," I countered. "Thought I'd better get that said before you did."

"All that money! When I think of what I could do right now with the 30 or 40 grand I spent on auditing, it makes me crazy."

"Yeah, but you have to admit, you made some good gains on the lower levels. Even if you hadn't said anything to me—which you did—I could see it made a positive difference—certainly at the beginning."

"You Scientologists thought you were the Chosen, didn't you? Marching to Hubbard's plan for The Master Race."

"Not exactly, but for a time, I did buy into the idea that we were saving the planet. Not quite sure what we were supposed to be saving it from, but…"

"From this point in time, it looks like Scientology succeeded in fucking it up even worse."

"You'll get no argument from me on that," I muttered, once again, hoping to change the subject. "Amazing how tall and how green the trees are in this area. Have you noticed?"

"Yes. Does that mean we're done talking about what a con Scientology turned out to be?"

"Apparently not. You remember when Yvonne Gilliam first informed me that Hubbard wanted to open a Celebrity Centre in Rome and I was the likely person to spearhead it? I asked you to consider joining me. You remember that?"

"How could I forget? The prospect of my leaving Tom for Rome put the fear of God in him. He was super nice to me for a long time after that."

"So how come you waited this long to tell me?"

"Tom never forgot that evening in our kitchen when you professed your unquestioning faith in Hubbard's outrageous theories. Tom asked you how you knew them to be true—how you could accept them as gospel and you answered 'Truth is self-evident. Truth presents itself as Maxims. Hubbard says if it isn't true for you, it isn't true. But his researches and conclusions ring true for me, therefore they are true." Clive commenced to laugh. "Maybe I didn't get every word right, but you know I'm damned close."

I was blushing. "A lot has changed since then," I admitted. "Scientology was originally presented as an applied philosophy. "The Science of Knowing How to Know," was its catchphrase. We were assured religion had no part in it, so I thought it was *the* path to enlightenment. When I cognited that…"

"Cognited? Isn't that one of Hubbard's made-up words?"

"It is. What I meant to say was, when I began to *grasp* that Scientology was a sinister exercise in self-hypnosis, I withdrew as quickly and as carefully as I could. I still have moments when I think maybe I didn't give it my all—didn't do the levels quite right—and may live to regret it. But that's the Catch 22 of Scientology, isn't it? The dangling carrot. 'You'll get what it's all about on the next level. Go directly to the cashier, give us every fucking dime you have and we just might let you in on the secrets of the universe—on a gradient, of course.'

"Gradient being Scientologese for 'It'll cost you big time, every time." Clive said.

"Still, I try not to sound too bitter. What's the point?"

"I have to admit, I'm proud of you. Not easy to withdraw from that evil cult—silently or noisily."

"I think one of the initial turning points for me was that time I was staying in your guest room at the Cordell Drive house. I was in the middle of a solo OT II session when Tom came bursting in with a pair of workmen in tow. I was sure some awful fate would befall me but despite my fears and dutifully reporting the incident to my case supervisor, nothing happened—good or bad. That was one of the early indicators that perhaps there was less to Scientology than met the eye."

"Say that out loud and they come after you, don't they?"

"And they have. Nasty phone calls. Dunning letters. Ordering friends to cut off all communication with me."

"You still get mail from them?"

"Last year I saved up a shoebox full of their promo, taped one of their postage-paid envelopes to it and shipped it back with a note, "This is my final request before I go to the authorities. Please stop wasting your money and my time. Take me off your mailing list once and for all. Totally off."

"Did it work?"

"A couple more pieces arrived after that, and then—I guess I finally got through to somebody."

"So many Scientologists bragged about recalling their past lives when they were in session," Clive said, barely suppressing a sneer. "Did that ever happen for you?"

"A couple of times."

"I get the concept, but, truthfully, it's never been very real for me," he admitted.

"I had several weird experiences as a little boy—none of which made any sense until I was an adult and began to apply the idea of past lives to them."

"You once told me you thought having lived before as a female could be an explanation for being Gay this lifetime? You still think that's true?"

"The theory goes that we've each been hero and villain, saint and sinner, rich and poor. Why not male and female?"

"You left out *rapist* and '*the raped*,' he said, "but you did get me to thinking. The idea of being hung up in a past life incident as a female doesn't seem so far fetched."

"What keeps me from dragging it into daily conversation is the fact that so many believers claim they were Jesus Christ or Madame Curé or…"

"…Abraham Lincoln or Amelia Earhart."

"Exactly! To hear them tell it, nobody was ever a peasant or a slave."

"Always a king or queen…"

I gestured to him. "I rest my case."

"Bitch! Tom and I discussed reincarnation on several occasions—trying to figure out how in the world two unlikelies like us had found each other, but he was easily bored and dismissed the whole idea as poppycock. "So what if I was Louis XIV or Napoleon Bonaparte," he said, "what the hell difference would that make?"

"I would have guessed Tom to be more of a Marie Antoinette."

"Not so far fetched. Might explain why he had a life-long pain in-the-neck."

"A pain in the neck doesn't automatically make you Marie Antoinette, but it is amusing to consider."

"We'll stay together as long as it feels good,' he would say. 'And when it doesn't any longer, we'll part. At that point, who we might have been in a past life won't make a damned bit of difference."

"Yet Tom's historical fiction was so detailed—so awesomely real, I can't see how he could have conjured all those vivid period images just from research."

"On that, I'll agree with you," Clive nodded.

"Can't say my auditing sessions were an absolute confirmation that it was all true, but, giving the devil his due, Level 5, so-called Power Processing—confirmed for me that I hadn't gone totally bonkers, and maybe I should stop being so defensive about my ability to recall the impossible."

"I've been on a parallel path for a long time," Clive sighed. "One that's pretty much without judgments and so forgiving, sometimes it doesn't even seem like a path."

"What path is that? Does it have a name?"

"Not really. It's a combination of several philosophies. All of them spiritual, none of them judgmental. Things I found that work for me—things that make me happy."

"For instance?"

"I went to see Lorena in Santa Monica on Thursday," he declared. "Figured she might have some helpful advice for this trip and a few clues about the months ahead."

"Forgive me, but who is Lorena?"

"I've mentioned her before. My sister recommended her to you the other night."

"Oh, you're talking about that spiritualist, but you never said her name before."

"I'm sure I did. Anyway, without my ever uttering a word, Lorena had plenty to say about this trip—and lots more about my upcoming time in the city." He glanced at me, as if anticipating I would challenge some part or all of what he was about to say.

"Happy for you. And since I'm not Lorena and don't have her powers, how many of her prognostications are you willing to share?"

"Your skepticism is flashing like a disco strobe. Have you ever been to a spiritualist?"

"No, not really. Closest I came was a tarot card reader on Jackson Square. It was Mardi Gras week and a friend and I were blissed-out on

Sazeracs on my balcony. He insisted on treating me to a reading. To say I was underwhelmed, would be putting it politely."

"Tarot cards have their place, but that's not the same as a full-fledged seer."

"Taking your word for it. So, what did Lorena predict?"

"Traffic would be intense, we should drive carefully, never take our eyes off the road, pull over when we feel sleepy, drink plenty of bottled water..."

"You sure you didn't have a *Triple A Travel Guide* sticking out of your pocket when you sat down with her?"

"What's the point of my telling you any more if that's your attitude?"

"What do Lorena's 'consultations' cost, if you don't mind my asking?"

"I do mind, but I also know when there's no stopping you."

"So, how much?"

"$50. for 30 minutes. $90. for an hour. You get a discount if you see her more than twice a year."

"And take out a second mortgage if you want to see her weekly."

"Now, just stop that! Her clients are some of the biggest names in the entertainment industry."

"Well, shut mah mouth. No arguing with that factoid. So what other astounding revelations did Mother Lorena unleash?"

"She said my sister and I were married in a past life."

"I could have told you that—for free."

"She also said to watch out for my travelling companion. He was a callous cunt who could quickly become a royal pain-in-the-ass."

"Lorena sounds very perceptive, not to mention classy."

"She is, but I have to correct one thing. Lorena is too much of a lady to use the word 'callous.' She called you a 'pretentious' cunt."

"Good for her. I crave precision in my epithets. They have so little sting without it."

"She said you and I would fight half of every day on the road, pretend to make it up for the other half and never once agree on where or what to eat."

"Too brilliant! Was this Lorena's $50. volume-rate revelation or her $90. luxury edition?"

"That doesn't deserve an answer. Look, it's 5:15 and we're both tired. That last sign said we're 40 miles outside Green River. See if there's a Motel 6 listed and give them a call."

Motel 6—Green River
1860 East Main Street
I-70 at Business Loop 70
Green River, UT, 84525
Phone: (435) 564-3436 (435) 564-3436

Welcome to Motel 6 Green River in Green River, Utah— conveniently located off the I-70 business loop. Features include outdoor seasonal pool, guest laundry facility, and micro fridge units in select rooms. WIFI in all rooms for *an* (sic) nominal fee.

We were seated at a weather-stained picnic table perched on the hillside behind the motel, the two dogs gamboled leash-less nearby. Clive poured a second generous Smirnoff into his plastic glass. It wasn't until then I noticed he hadn't bothered to take the cellophane off it.

"How can you drink that without ice?" I griped. "I'll go find the machine and get you some."

"It's alright," he shrugged. "I'm fine. Waiting for the click. You know what's meant by 'the click?'"

I nodded and raised my glass. "Anyone who's ever devoted any serious time to drinking knows about the click," I said, holding my Chardonnay aloft to catch the sun's slanting rays. "First heard it when Tennessee Williams had Geraldine Page's character say it in "Sweet Bird of Youth.""

"Right on the playwright, wrong on the play, C. Bobby. It's one of Paul Newman's lines as Brick in "Cat On A Hot Tin Roof.""

"You're absolutely right. Must be having a brain fart."

"Tom hated that expression. So do I. We thought it was too vulgar."

"Mea culpa, Mother Abbess. How about 'Senior moment?'"

"Better," he smiled and stared at the Smirnoff label. "The click's a wonderful thing, but, I have to admit, it's becoming more and more elusive."

"Maybe it only works with bourbon. What the hell would Russians know about a click, anyway? Every Russian I've ever known deserved a *kick* in the head, not a click."

"Oh, that's clever, C. Bob! How many Russians have you known, anyway? No, don't tell me now. Save it for the morning when I can alert the media." He cupped his hand to his forehead to shield the blazing sunset. "Red sky at night, sailor's delight. Red sky in morning, sailor's warning." He tossed back the glass. "Shit! I think I just missed the click," he gasped and poured another. "Just have to try again—maybe sneak up on it, this time."

Back in the room, I turned on the TV to watch the first installment of a Biblical mini-series that a friend had directed in Italy. Despite its lavish production values and my admiration for his work, the fuzzy picture, tinny sound and my overwhelming exhaustion made me turn it off after 10 minutes. Guilt for not having watched all of it, stayed with me for some time.

Day Three

We gobbled down our complimentary 'continental' breakfast (orange colored liquid, Saran-wrapped sticky bun, instant coffee) to get an early start. Our good intentions were momentarily rattled when Clive noticed the clock on an old bank building read 12:15.

"Jesus! Did we oversleep?" he asked.

"Doesn't seem possible," I answered as I checked my cell phone. "And, it isn't. It's 8:30—exactly." A closer look at the sign on the boarded up building revealed it was for sale, and, judging by the amount of pigeon droppings and spray-can graffiti blanketing it, must have been for a long time.

Since it was my turn at the wheel, I suggested we should try for a 700 mile day, explaining that's how I used to divide up my three day, 1900 mile, LA to New Orleans trips: 700, 700 and 500 miles. "So, if I could do it alone, certainly the two of us can make it happen."

"Let's do it! 700 miles ought to put us over the Nebraska border. Think we can make it before sunset?"

"For the record, I'm setting cruise control at 73," I declared. "And get ready to hide that damned radar detector the minute we see anything that resembles flashing lights."

"Worry wort! If it makes you feel any better, I'll unplug it and only use it when I'm driving."

"How's this for when we're pulled over? 'I swear I knew nothing about it, Officer. I thought it was his Walkman."

"He'll know you're full of shit. Nobody uses a Walkman any more—they all have iPods. Even in Bum Fuck, Utah."

"Nevertheless, indulge my paranoia. Put the goddam thing away." Which, to his credit, he did by placing the device in a zip-lock bag and, after discovering there was no space left in the glove compartment, shoved it under the passenger seat.

"That works. Thank you, Clive."

"Speaking of work, I was reminiscing with my sister about our childhood a few weeks ago and we figured out I've been working for a living since I was ten years old."

"Makes two of us," I said, stifling a yawn. "Part of the era we grew up in. 'You kids need to learn the value of a dollar,' is how my Mother used to put it."

"I mean, actually working—earning money," Clive countered. "Money doesn't grow on trees,' was Eva's favorite expression. So she had me singing and tap dancing under the palmettos in the town square in Port-of-Spain. I remember staring up at those huge fronds, hoping to prove her wrong."

"Sounds like more fun than what my Mother had me doing—picking blueberries on a farm, eight hours a day. It was run by four rabidly Baptist brothers named Cutts, which is kind of onomatopoeic, now that I'm thinking about it. The Cutts brothers paid us a nickel a pint. If you worked like a demon—made sure there weren't any green or dead berries in the tray—a tray held twelve pints—you could bring home $3.60 a day."

"But you didn't have to wear lipstick and rouge and sing "Puttin' On The Ritz."

"True, but we did wear Calamine and oil of Citronella to repel the mosquitoes." I pondered for a moment. "Jesus, Citronella had an awful smell! Just saying the word brings it back."

"We wore Citronella, too—underneath the lipstick and rouge. Had to. Anybody who's ever been to Trinidad knows the mosquitoes are bigger than cicadas."

"I see we've entered a hyperbole duel. Very well, I'll allow your cicada-sized mosquitoes if you'll let me introduce my cotton-mouthed adders—the snakes that occasionally slithered their way into the patches and sent the womenfolk screaming to the packing sheds."

"*So C. Bobby*! Turn everything into a competition, even if you have to drag in snakes to do it."

"Actually, if you recall, I said, 'Slithered in.' Perhaps I should have said 'rhumbaed in?' Anyway, it really did happen. Scared the hell out of everybody. One of the Cutts brothers, I think his name was Orville, was the chief snake wrangler. He'd catch the adders with a rake and machete their heads off. We ten-year-olds thought that was so cool. Then he'd skin them and hang them up to dry outside the loading docks. Rumor had it the Cutts brothers made Sunday-go-to-church belts out of them, but I never saw one, so I couldn't confirm it."

"Okay, you win. Snakes trump tap-dancing and eye-shadow, every time. But you're going to hear the rest of my story, anyway."

"Who's stopping you?"

"After I finished my song and dance act—with my sister and two older brothers as backup singers, Mom made me pass around my little top hat. If that didn't go well, she and my Step-Dad would take over and harass the crowd into coughing up a Trinidad and Tobago dollar or two. Jesus, how that embarrassed me! Even now, makes me blush just to tell you about it."

"Stage Mothers have no shame. Never have—never will. That's why *Momma Rose* in 'Gypsy' packs such a wallop. Mine, on the other hand, while no Stage Mother, was equally determined I learn the value of dollar, and, from age 10, had me earn money to pay for my school clothes."

Clive gave me what I'd long ago labeled his 'condescending glance of appraisal.'

"Just proves that it's never too early to instill a true fashion sense," he sniffed. "Go back in the house, take off any three things…"

"…and you'll still be over-dressed," I completed his favorite fashion gag. "You have any idea how many years ago you first said that to me?"

"No, but I gather you're about to tell me."

"Try 25. And how many times you've repeated it, since?"

"Classic style never grows old," he sniffed.

"Thank you, Anna Wintour. I'll have you know, I ordered my school ensembles from the Montgomery Ward catalogue. High-end compared to the Sears Roebuck catalogue, which I hear was all the rage with the proletariat in Trinidad."

"True, but it was the only choice we had—until we moved to Toronto. Then Eva trotted us down to Eaton's once a month. Eaton's was referred to as the Sax Fifth Avenue of Canada. She did this even though we couldn't afford to buy anything, but it was fun to look."

"Mother would nag Daddy to take us to Wanamaker's in Philadelphia—always a thrill for me. It felt like visiting a palace. We never bought anything either, but Mother claimed that 'window-shopping' through Wanamaker's eight or nine floors gave her some good ideas."

"Like Eaton's did for Mom. My brothers hated everything about those trips. They hated being my back-up singers in Trinidad and hated having to play second-fiddle to Mom's show-biz aspirations for me in Toronto. Only my sister put up with it 'cause she and I were inseparable."

"You do look like twins."

"Everybody assumes we are. But there's a three year difference."

"Which way?"

"How would knowing that make your life any better?" he asked, somewhat churlishly.

"Saves me having to count the rings under your bark," I said.

"I don't have bark. Dr. Fournier removed it all while I was 'on holiday' in Costa Rica. Remember?"

"Forgive me. I'd forgotten to notice. I gather you're not going to answer the age question, even though I've already figured it out."

"Younger! She's three years younger! Now, do you feel better?"

"Much. And thank you for your candor, which I realize, is not something you readily dispense."

"No, but I could readily dispense a smack up the side of your head if you'd lean this way for a second."

"Can't. Too busy counting spotted cows. Up to 36 already and we're still in Colorado."

"You're mad as a hatter, Holloway."

Pow! Pshhhhhhhhhh! Thump! Thump! Thump! Suddenly, the vehicle was veering wildly to the left, threatening to pull us into the westbound lane filled with an unending caravan of 18 wheelers. Clive instinctively turned on the emergency flashers and called out, "Pull right, pull right."

"I can't! Not yet! There's a humongous truck right behind us."

"He's slowing down! He's slowing down! Must have figured out the problem. Here, I'll help you." Clive grabbed the wheel and together we steered the Rover onto the right shoulder. It was a blowout and a serious one. Neither of us were experienced mechanics, despite bragging about having changed a tire or two. My big concern was whether or not the rim had been bent. "Good thing the spare is bolted to the back hatch and not buried under the floor boards," I said.

"Unfortunately, the jack and lug wrench are," Clive sighed. "Not to panic. We'll put the dogs in the front seat, prop up as much as we can with a couple of those big rocks over there, and I'll fish the damned things out."

"Hope the spare is in good shape and properly inflated?"

"It better be. I had my Malibu mechanic check out everything a couple of days before we left."

There's always an element of danger whenever a vehicle is disabled alongside a super highway, but changing a tire so close to a steady stream of roaring trucks and speeding cars proved quite unnerving. After turning the last lug nut, replacing the hubcap and strapping the ruined tire to the roof, we were both sweating, despite the morning chill. Before we resumed, I glanced at the map. "The next major town is Idaho Springs. I say, when we get there, first thing we do is find a tire store and replace the spare, and then look for some lunch."

"I'm guessing the tire's going to be expensive in these parts."

"I'll go halves with you, Clive. I'm not willing to risk the rest of the trip without a spare." Realizing the existing spare was not fully inflated, we crept into Idaho Springs where a State Trooper kindly directed us to Allied Towing, who's titillating slogan, 'We offer more than just towing' proved to be accurate. It was easy to restrain my temptation to ask Wilbur, the handsome young man behind the counter, to define exactly what is 'more than just towing,' when he told us the spare would 'run ya' about $200. plus tax and we have to bring it from our warehouse.' "Is there nothing cheaper?" I asked, somewhat taken aback.

When he answered, "Not in that size, not for that model. Sorry," we had no choice but to take Wilber at his word. After a beat, I decided, "Nothing to do but to do it. Here, put it on my debit card," and handed it to Wilbur.

"Thanks, C. R.," Clive whispered, clearly relieved. "I'll work out splitting it with you, later."

"In the meantime, we're starving, Wilbur. We'll leave the rim with you while we go for some lunch. Can you recommend anything? Preferably a place that serves food indigenous to the area?"

"If you like chili, best place in town is called Kermitt's, about ten minutes from here. I can show you on the map."

"Great." I looked at Clive who shrugged, indifferently. "We're both crazy about chili, aren't we, Clive?"

"Perfect for a long car ride," he answered, which made Wilbur smile.

"Kermitt's chili is the only one in town that doesn't give ya gas," he said, proudly. "He claims to use a magic ingredient."

"Gasless chili. And in Colorado, of all places." Clive shook his head. "Who would have thunk it?"

Source: www.kermitts.com

We were immediately encouraged on seeing the scores of dollar bills and business cards pinned to Kermitt's walls and ceilings. A street sign over the bar proclaiming 'Bullshit Blvd,' confirmed that it was the perfect spot for two iconoclastic smart asses. As promised, the bowls of chili were generous, the flavor robust and spicy. However, for a sprawling, rustic establishment, plastered with bawdy sign-boards in every corner, the patrons seemed surprisingly dour. Perhaps I shouldn't have brought it up, but I couldn't resist. The sullen crowd looked like it might benefit by witnessing someone else having a good laugh.

"How's that line go again?" I asked Clive. "Between Maria and the Mother Superior in "The Sound of Music?"

"Hardly the time or place for that story."

"Why not? The Rockies sort of resemble the Alps, don't you think?" The sly look of a mischievous little boy who's about to say something wicked and fairly sure he'll get away with it, came over Clive's face.

"It's just before the first act finale," he whispered, when the Mother Superior sings 'Climb Every Mountain.' It was Tom's all time favorite theatre story."

"You'd think I'd remember it, as many times as you've told it," I confessed, already giggling in anticipation. "It cracks me up so badly, I can never remember the exact wording."

"Tom knew Patricia Neway, who played the Mother Superior. He said she had a wicked sense of humor and never let the producers forget she was a real opera diva and what a favor she was doing them by 'slumming' in a Broadway musical."

"Wasn't Mary Martin's husband one of the producers?"

"Yeah, Richard Halliday. They say he and Martin weren't exactly aspirins to work with, either."

"So, tell me, tell me, tell me—how does the line go again?"

"Maria is having doubts about completing her obligations as a novitiate—she's been working for Baron von Trapp and his kids, away from the convent and having un-nun-like thoughts. She says to the Mother Superior, "I have doubts. I'm not sure I'm meant for this life, Reverend Mother.""

"It's coming back. Hurry up, before I pee my pants."

"Tom claimed that the stagehands and chorus members gathered in the wings every night just to hear Neway say the line."

"Which is....?"

"...Supposed to be 'What is it you can't face, Maria?' but with Neway's operatic pronunciation it came out, "What is it you *cunt* face, Maria!"

As happened so many times before, we howled ourselves into tears, leaving no choice but to bury our faces in our napkins and race to the men's room for relief. When we returned to our table, our waitress asked what in the world was so funny and could we tell her, 'cause she 'needed a good laugh.' I fibbed and told her it was an old family joke, and wouldn't survive the retelling. The lunch tab came to a hefty $30. with tip, but we were rejuvenated and more resolved than ever to make our 700 mile goal.

As we jogged to the parking lot, Clive choked out, "Never ask me to tell that in public again. We could have gotten in all kinds of trouble. Most women hate the 'C' word."

"And the Brits love it," I shot back. On our arrival at Allied Towing, Wilbur had the spare ready and personally hitched it to the rear gate. We shouted our thanks and were once again on our way. With Clive at the wheel, that meant frequently pushing the speed limit.

Once again, it was time to refuel the Rover and just ahead was the town of Ft. Morgan. I loved the name because it sounded like the title of a serialized Western from the Saturday matinees of my childhood. We pulled off Hwy 70 into the USA Gas Station, for our fourth fill-up @ $66.00.

"What's with you decorator types?" I groused. "Driving these huge vehicles? Seems every one I've ever known, male or female, straight or gay, drives some kind of four wheel drive like a Jeep or Land Rover or an Escalade—and lately, I've been seeing more and more Hummers."

"What's with your judgmental tone? You about to deliver a lecture on global warming?"

"No lecture, but it strikes me as weird why you Design Fairies need a four wheel drive to haul a lamp or an end table up to the Hollywood Hills. Not exactly like crossing the Matterhorn in a blizzard, is it?"

"Not at all judgmental, are we? Am I supposed to feel defensive about what decorators drive?"

"Seems ridiculously expensive, that's all. Witness what we just paid filling up this monster. Beyond that—and I hope you won't take this as personally insulting—but driving a gigantic SUV strikes me as classic compensation for penis-envy."

"Oh it does, does it? Well, Dr. Freud, if you'll set your clichéd theory aside for a minute, I'll try to clue you in. At the start of the job, the client always wants to see tons of choices. We have to drag around samples of flooring, tile samples, fabric swatches, wall treatments, catalogues of lighting fixtures, Polaroids of furniture—you name it. And often, near the end of a job, there are odds and ends of furniture, art, plants, urns, flower arrangements and various accessories that I need to pick up at the last minute. Try squeezing all that stuff into a VW Beetle, Sigmund."

"All well and good, but now that you're no longer in the business, why hold onto the Rover? And in New York City, for Christ's sake?"

"I owe several more payments on it, for one thing. Don't worry, after I get settled in, I'll be storing it at Jennifer's place—up in Katonah."

"Who's Jennifer and where's Katonah?"

"You'll find out when we drive up on Sunday."

"We're back in the Rover the day after we arrive?" I groaned, not bothering to hide my displeasure.

"I told you that several days ago. I have to retrieve a few things."

"Oh, joy! I can hardly wait to spend another day strapped in this van."

"Relax, Mary. Katonah is just up the Expressway—less than an hour from the city."

My ears became increasingly plugged as we ascended Interstate 70 to 11,000 feet and were about to enter the amazing Eisenhower Tunnel, sixty miles West of Denver. I was marveling at how clean its porcelain tiles were, compared to the Lincoln and Holland Tunnels when Clive mumbled something that sounded like a riddle.

"Sorry, I can't hear you." I tapped my ear. "Could you say it again?"

"Ever thought about doing a *Thelma and Louise*?" he shouted.

"Can't say that I have," I yelled back. "Feels like we're on a fairly steep grade. Shouldn't you slow down a bit?" Either he hadn't heard me or chose not to.

"I've been mulling over a concept for a sequel," he yelled. "A male version."

"You mean with two gay men? Sounds like just what the macho movie-going public has been waiting for."

"No, Larry Kramer, the guys don't have to be queer. Just good buddies and simpatico with each other over the crappy way their lives have turned out and want to be together to the end."

"So you've given this some serious thought?"

He nodded. "I'm just spit-balling here, but how about if somehow the husband and the rapist from the original *Thelma and Louise* got together?"

"Certainly would redefine *Bromance,*" I called out.

"I can't tell if you're being serious or a vicious cunt."

I gestured to an overhead sign indicating 1000 feet to the end of the tunnel and screamed, "If you slow down, I'll give you my answer."

"I don't see what that has to do with it," he shouted, but since we were roaring down a palpable gradient inside what resembled the bore of a giant cannon, he dropped into 2nd gear.

"Thank you. My family thanks you. My creditors thank you. Now, how's this for a title? *Telemachus and Louie!*"

He pondered for a moment. "Too hard to spell—too hard to pronounce. Tom used to say, 'if you can't envision it on a small-town marquee, don't imagine it.' Now, are you being serious or not?"

"Just trying to envision the arc. Screenplay 101—always have to have an arc. These days, the steeper the better." With that, we shot from the tunnel, with only a stubby cable fence shielding us from catapulting over the two mile high cliff.

"So let me understand," I said, relieved that he was keeping the Rover in low gear for the time being. "You're thinking the guys' motivation for driving over the cliff would be their realization that their lives had turned to meaningless shit or because of the pain they'd caused Thelma and Louise?"

"Maybe both, but you wouldn't need to spell it out that blatantly," he yelled before realizing he could resume speaking in a normal tone. "There could be several motivations. Leave it to the audience to pick the one that resonates for them."

I allowed a pointed silence to pass while trying to come up with a constructive evaluation. In hindsight, it wasn't my most diplomatic moment. "Haven't we always promised each other to be blunt—not play patty-cake over our literary efforts?"

"That means you hate it, right?"

"Well, as we used to say in the Location Scouting business, 'I don't want to be a dream-stomper,' but I think it's a totally unworkable idea."

"Maybe over dinner you'll tell me what you really think?"

"Notice I stopped just this side of *imbecilic*."

"What a mean, shitty thing to say. No wonder you and I have never had a successful collaboration." Maggie and Georgie started whining and Clive's cell phone chimed from his multi-pocketed windbreaker.

"The next Rest Stop is 30 some miles ahead," I cautioned. "I think we should pull into that runaway-emergency turn off. I'll handle the dogs so you can answer that call."

He was seething. "That's the first non-cunty thing you've said all day." Clearly, I had touched a very sore spot.

"I'm sorry and I apologize. Sometimes my idea of humor gets lost in the phrasing." He brought the Rover to a halt, located his phone and stepped from the vehicle.

"Put their leashes on before you let them out," he snapped. "The poop bags are in the glove compartment."

"I know the drill, Sargeant," I whispered, bowing low.

"I'll accept your apology *after you buy dinner tonight*, but I continue to think you're a vindictive cunt."

"And what do *you* think, Maggie—Georgie?" I asked, as I reached for their collars and snapped their leashes in place. "Is that so? I'll tell your Daddy. Clive, the girls are saying, if the merkin fits, I deserve to wear it."

After determining his call was from Macy's in New York, he signaled for me to stand next to him. "It's about the mattress delivery.

Quick, write these numbers down, Bob." (It should be noted that Clive only called me Bob when he was seriously pissed with me) "It's the confirmation number." Then, on the phone, "Say it again, please? 1945957." After I dutifully inked the numbers into my Daytimer, he handed me the phone so I could read them back to the operator, but we lost the signal before I was finished. Walking back to the Rover, he said, "If the mattresses haven't arrived by Saturday, I'm supposed to call them and give them that number. So, please don't lose it, Bob."

"Don't worry, Your Majesty. Bob won't lose it because *C. Robert* put it into his trusty Daytimer."

"We are not amused," he sniffed, though I sensed the ice had begun to thaw shortly after we soared past the shimmering towers of Valhalla-like Denver, preening through the clouds that forever swirl across its mile-high plateau.

We drove for several minutes without a word being exchanged. I was mentally drafting some form of an apology, when he surprised me by asking, "Did you ever read *Young Man from the Provinces,* by Alan Helm?"

"Yes. I think you bought it for me."

"Did I? Confirms how much I loved it. So well written."

"I did too. What an arc! From being labeled 'the best piece of ass in New York City' to becoming Visconti and Zeffirelli's boytoy in Rome to…"

"…teaching English Lit at Columbia University. What a life, indeed!" Clive sighed.

"He recounted the New York gay demimonde of the 50s and 60s better than anyone has done before or since."

"How would you know?" Clive challenged me.

"That's my era. I came to New York in the mid 50s, right out of high school, ready to conquer Broadway. I was about to turn 18, fearless and hopelessly naïve."

"I knew Alan, you know. We had a brief fling—God he was sexy then! From his picture on the dust jacket, looks like he's lost all his hair, but still…"

I flipped down the visor and checked my hair in the mirror. "He wrote quite movingly about how difficult aging can be for gay men."

"Especially if we don't make every effort to keep ourselves in shape, C. Bobby. You really ought to give some thought to losing 20–25 pounds."

"So right. Remind me the next time you pull us into a Dairy Queen."

"Alan's book really inspired me. I've been thinking—maybe I should write about my life. It's been pretty amazing, looking back."

"I'm guessing the only one stopping you is you?"

"Been involved with some incredible men over the years. Wasn't just Tom, you know?"

"I'd like to think I was one of them."

"You were—are—but not that way. I'm talking sexually—romantically."

"Do I hear a notched-belt about to be unbuckled?"

"Quick, let me write that down."

"And I'll write down the names you're about to reveal. Fair enough?"

"No, you won't—if I ask you not to."

"You're right. So where are we headed with this?"

"How many people can claim they had a fling with Rock Hudson and Tab Hunter, in the same year?"

"So *it is* a notched belt I'm seeing—and not merely Asbury Park."

"Insufferable! Then there was Michael Bennett. 'Course I was just another trophy for him—which wasn't so bad because later on, he hired me to decorate his East Side penthouse."

"You never mentioned Bennett before. Must have been tricky, banging the boss and all that?"

"It was a fair trade. I wanted to play 'Zack' in the touring company and he wanted entrée to Tom to make a musical out of one of the stories in *Crowned Heads*."

"Lucy *was* juicy. Sondheim got it right in *Follies*."

"Never made it with Sondheim. But Terrence McNally and I had a brief fling a hundred years ago when we were both young and pretty. A couple years back, we ran into each other at an opening night party and tried again. He's a very sweet, very talented man, but I wasn't ready to be Mrs. McNally. Weekdays in Manhattan, weekends on Long Island—I'm not made that way."

"Here's to the ladies who lunch. Dinosaurs surviving the crunch. I'll drink to that!"

"I don't think it was going to be that bad…"

The dogs commenced to whine—clear signal they hated my singing or needed a rest stop, or both. "What I'm hearing is, you're still looking for someone to replace Tom."

He shrugged, signaling a calculated indifference. "I think it's time for you to take over, after the next stop, C. Bobby."

"Whatever happened to that guy who was your partner in the decorating business—the one you asked me to give a loan to?" I asked. "I've forgotten his name?"

"You mean Joshua? After I dissolved the business, we cut all communication. Last I heard he was very sick—not expected to make it."

"But you guys were so successful. Made the cover of *Architectural Digest*, didn't you?"

"*We* didn't, but I did, twice, you'll remember. Joshua was a piece of work. Talented—had a gift for gab; our female clients loved him but he was always in trouble with money. Overbilling, squandering their deposits before he actually ordered anything from the suppliers."

"Let me guess? He was having breakfast off a mirror and lunch through a rolled up twenty."

"You left out 'dinner from a pipe.' Where did you learn those quaint phrases?"

"Movies. The Internet. Observing film crews. So, am I right?"

"Everybody was doing it. Even our clients. Some of us knew when to stop, some of us couldn't."

"I saw enough of it in the film biz. Directors and producers tooting up first thing in the morning, before climbing in the van for a location scout. Hated the effect it had on them. Even more, I hated how they treated me and my staff when they were stoned. Talked a mile a minute—gave directions that didn't make any sense, dismissed perfect locations without getting out of the van to look at them. Don't ask what that did to the shooting schedule."

"Okay, I won't."

"Thank God, I never got into it. I guess I have Scientology to thank for that."

"Really?" Clive sniffed. "You'd be hard pressed to say which was the more expensive habit."

"The only time I ever did cocaine was with you—at Hedges Way. Remember? We were talking about it and you showed me what it looked like—you had it hidden in a caper jar in your refrigerator."

He nodded. "You kept saying you weren't feeling anything and took several more toots."

"Then, that good-looking tenant of yours appeared from upstairs, wanting to know what all the noise was about."

"That was Matt and by the time he arrived, you'd snorted it all, so he couldn't join in the fun."

"We decided to adjourn to that bar on Melrose—remember? The one with the fire-pit in the back?"

"All the bars on Melrose had fire-pits in the back. I warned you that Matt was straight, but that didn't stop you hitting on him like a rhino in heat."

"I did not hit on him! I have perfect Gaydar."

"Did too! While you were trying to stick your tongue in his ear, you whispered, "It's okay, Matt. Everybody's a little bit straight.""

"Usually gets a big laugh. Kept me out of a serious trouble on more than one occasion."

"Yeah, well I think my being his landlord kept him from punching you out that night."

"Probably. Which reminds me—I've never properly thanked you for the experience."

"You being the 'C' word again?"

"Am not. Take the win and be grateful. Doing cocaine with someone I trusted completely, took all the mystery out of it. I already behaved like I was permanently on Speed. Cocaine made me go even faster—made me think I was smarter than anyone around—which is exactly what I'd been seeing in all those producer types."

"Doesn't do that for everyone."

"Au contraire, it pretty much does. 'I am God and you all are mere mortals—my serfs. Harken ye to my brilliance!' Worse, I suffered a terrible hangover afterwards—migraine headache kind of hangover. Lasted for two or three days."

"That never happened to me," Clive said, looking aside to punctuate his claim.

"So, my second over-due thank you is for giving me an up close and in-person experience I never wanted to repeat. I've always been high on life. Figure it's about the strongest drug I can handle."

"When did this become an AA meeting?"

"Now who's being a 'C' word? My testament usually gets big applause at Alanon meetings."

"Given your Diva delivery, I'm not surprised."

"Don't know about you," I said, "but I always find it a bit upsetting when some of my closest friends don't like each other, especially when they're vocal about it."

"Easy enough. Don't listen to them," Clive muttered.

"Case in point: When I bragged about my longtime friendship with you to Joe Hardy, the director, he asked me, 'What do you two do together—each other's nails?"

"That's his Old-Queen envy showing. Nothing good to take away from that story. Why are you bothering to repeat it?"

"Equally perplexing is when I realize not all my close friend's friends like me."

"The curse of the social animal—or the paranoid. Learn to live with it, or get like me and no longer give a damn about other people's opinions."

"Brave talk, Cliveo, but I find that hard to believe. When you had your showing at that gallery in New York, you emailed me the reviews—mostly raves, as I recall. Would you have bothered if they hadn't been?"

Clive broke into his second real smile of the day. "Ah, yes—the Wickiser Gallery. Very prestigious. Walter Wickiser is so respected, when he shows an artist, it all but guarantees the critics will write a good review."

"Which speaks to the quality of your work, but the question remains, what if the critics hadn't been so kind? You still maintain you wouldn't give a damn?"

"That's mixing apples and oranges. Certainly critic's opinions matter—especially to an artist. But some bitter Queen's bitchy judgment of me personally, doesn't matter for shit. Tom taught me a long time ago, let idle gossip get to you and sooner or later, you'll want to kill yourself."

"Interesting. Does that explain why you seem overly-possessive about your circle of friends?"

"What's that supposed to mean?"

"Seems like you clutch them to your chest like cards in a poker game."

"Really! Have you ever considered I might have a sixth sense about who might appreciate each other and who might not?"

"If that's your justification for wanting to know who was on the guest list before you'd accept an invitation to my parties, it's kind of wimpy. Whether it was for dinner, cocktails, or whatever, if you didn't know someone or didn't like someone, you declined with the excuse, "They make my fillings ring.""

"And some of them still do," he sneered. "Like that guy you used to write with…"

"No need to go there," I stopped him. "Bringing Richard up just proves my point. Once you've fixed an opinion on someone, there's no changing it. For your info, Richard holds a vaguely begrudging estimation of you, and, for the life of me, I can't tell you why."

"Nor would I care to know."

"Same anomaly applies to my friends Robert and Gerhard. Robert's one of my closest friends in the world, yet he's always covertly critical when he speaks of you."

"Now, that does surprise me. We barely know each other."

"You met my gorgeous friend, Gerhard, that first time he visited me from Capetown. You and Tom cooked us a lobster dinner and after a delightful evening, all you could say was 'He should be careful. Blondes always lose their hair early.' I mean, what kind of an assessment was that? Were you jealous of his stature and beauty or was it my unorthodox friendship with so stunning a man that upset you?"

"I won't dignify that with an answer. I'm guessing they put some kind of redneck truth serum in Kermitt's chili." He turned and stared out his window intently. "I don't think we need to go any further with this discussion."

"Fine. We've crossed the Nebraska border. Map says it's 602 miles from Green River to North Platte. I think that's close enough to our 700 mile goal, don't you?"

"Here's my phone. You know the drill. Make the call."

Motel 6, North Platte, NB 1 stars 1520 S JEFFERS ST, I-80 AT EXIT #177, NORTH PLATTE, NE 69101

Source: www.motel6.com

This Motel 6 offers a wide variety of amenities including: 24-hour front desk service, facilities for persons with disabilities and complimentary coffee. For a nominal charge fax services are available. Snack, beverage and ice centers are available. We offer several room types including rooms with one or two beds. I-80 Exit 177.

"Maybe it's time for a time out," I suggested. "I do this with Joe, my lawyer, whenever our discussions cut too close to the bone and..."

Clive interrupted. "How about when you pontificate in sweeping generalities that have little basis in fact?"

"If that's the way you see it. Just for tonight, why don't we take separate rooms?," I suggested. "Take a little break from each other—give each other some space? What do you say?"

"I say that's silly and a waste of money. How about we agree to stop scraping old scabs and stick to talking about the weather?"

"Now, *you're* sounding like an old fart. Tell you what, when we check in, we'll each get our own room key. Then I'll go for a long walk while it's still light—get something to eat at one of the fine dining spots sure to be surrounding the motel—and I suggest you do the same."

"Sounds like overkill, but maybe it's not such a bad idea. Only with our luck, we'll both end up at KFC."

"No, for the sake of our friendship, I'll deprive myself for one night. I've set my sights on Arby's."

When I returned to the room around 8:30, Clive was already in bed, with Maggie and Georgie snuggled around him. As I leaned to buss him on the forehead, Maggie growled slightly. Keeping his eyes closed, Clive whispered, 'It's okay, Maggie. C. Bobby promised not to be mean to me anymore."

Day Four

Wednesday, May 18th—North Platte, NB to

Clive was still sleeping when and I left the room for a solo breakfast at Roger's Café, a Mom and Pop establishment within easy walking distance. I splurged on a 'grand slam' breakfast and the tab came to a hefty $9.00. Walking back to the 6, I noticed a slightly more upscale inn, obviously locally owned, advertising free WiFi on its marquee. I entered the lobby, explained that I was staying down the street and asked if I might pay to have access. The kindly clerk said that wouldn't be necessary, handed me a slip of paper containing the access code and assured me I could sit anywhere in the lobby and get a signal. I did, and made note of the clerk's name and the Motel's address, so as to write a thank you when I got home.

After reading and answering several emails, I attempted to call my Mother, but her answering machine was turned off. As she is possessor of an infallible green thumb, I assumed she was in the backyard, working her flower beds.

Clive groaned from his bed when he heard me enter the room, "My God, look at the time! Why didn't you wake me?"

"Thought you needed the rest. Particularly after our little wrangle last night."

"What are you talking about?" he snapped as he leapt up and headed for the john.

"Doesn't matter. I found a cute place down the street and treated myself to a comfort-food breakfast. Afterwards, the motel next to it let me use their WiFi, for free."

"Happy for you, but we gotta get crackin.' I'll skip the shower and do a whore's bath—if you'll walk the girls…"

"…and put our bags in the van. But you'd best put something in your stomach before we set out."

"A cup of hot Valium would suit me just fine." Instead, he made do with a yogurt and an apple from a nearby Kwik Stop, making 10:45 our latest leave time on the trip. As was his want, Clive assumed the morning shift at the wheel. He seemed unusually muted for the first hour, so I took the opportunity to review my notes and prioritize tasks needing immediate attention.

Finally, Clive spoke. "I know you're a fan of Gore Vidal's."

"Indeed, I am. But, I have to ask, are you always this oblique in the morning?"

"No, but I've been thinking about our conversation last night and the deleterious effect Vidal's had on my life."

"Wow! That's an awfully steep tangent for this talk show host to moderate."

"You're right. Sorry I brought it up."

"Don't be. I'm intrigued. I consider Gore Vidal a true genius. And what a body of work! Self-taught—prep school, no formal college. It was because of Vidal I learned the definition of *Autodidact*."

"Good word. You consider yourself an Autodidact?"

"I do and that's probably why I identify with him so emphatically."

"You know, he and Tom were on friendly terms. We had dinner with him several times—but he was so caustic, I was always a little afraid of him."

"You got to sit at table with Gore Vidal? I envy you!"

"At one of our parties, he declared that the four most beautiful words in our language were 'I told you so.' Everybody laughed but me."

"Why? Who do you know who hasn't uttered a version of that, at one time or another?"

"If I did, I tried never to say it again after that night. He really rattled me when he said, 'It is not enough to succeed. Others must fail."

"He also said, 'Every time a friend succeeds, I die a little,' but that's the nature of ironic epigrams," I said, "turning Christian dogma and Reader's Digest homilies on their heads. Surely, you saw the genius in it, if not the humor?"

"I didn't at the time."

"Okay, but I'm still not sure where you're headed with this."

"I was 18 or 19. Hearing that other people had to fail for me to succeed—and when a friend succeeded, I was going to be so envious I'd feel bad about myself—coming from someone who was held in great esteem by everybody in the room—it was very confusing. It had a profound effect on me."

"*Profound effect* as in recognizing the universal truths in what Vidal was saying—that they could apply to everyone or resisting the idea that they might specifically apply to you?"

"There's a mouthful. But it doesn't speak to my point. If having a career as a performer meant having to be a cutthroat; living with envy and vengeful thoughts every day, I wanted no part of it. Nevertheless, when I turned 21, I found myself holding many of those exact same thoughts, and I hated the feeling. I've never forgiven Vidal for putting them in my head in the first place."

"Got it. Got it. Got it." I mimed picking up a hand mike. "And we thank you for sharing your heart-felt story with us, Mr. Wilson. After the commercial break, you won't want to miss our other guest, the celebrated author and raconteur, known for his acerbic observations on the Hollywood scene, a true national treasure, Mr. Gore Vidal will be right here in our studio."

Clive mimed grabbing the mike from me. "And right after that, Chef Wolfgang Puck is going to show us how to sauté Mountain Oysters using your host's very own scrotum. You won't want to miss that, either."

Somewhere west of Lincoln, Nebraska, my cell phone rang. Seeing "Caller Unknown" on its tiny screen, I first thought it could be Ronnie, up to one of his fiendish tricks, but realizing any number of concerned friends might be trying to reach me at this critical time, I decided to take a chance and answer it. It was someone identifying himself only as 'Eric,' an agent with Wells Fargo collection bureau. The bank was willing to settle my credit card debt at a favorable discount, if I agreed to pay in full right away. When I explained I was in a van travelling cross-country and wouldn't be able to do anything for a week or so, 'Eric' offered to speak to his supervisor about 'holding the deal for another week, but not a day longer.' He gave me an address where checks were to be mailed, and in a bizarre coincidence, the firm was located in the suburbs of Lincoln! I made 'Eric' laugh when I suggested he should look out his window and wave at us as we flew by. His personable tone made it possible to haggle him down from $15,185. to the discounted amount of $10,650. or four monthly payments of $2,662.50. When I suggested two payments of

$5,000. each, he said I was pushing my luck, but if I absolutely kept my word and he was in receipt of two cashier's checks by June 30th, he'd do his gosh-darnedest to make it work. "Golly! I can't ask for any more than that," I replied in my best 'grateful-golly-whiz' intonation.

After I hung up, Clive asked in amazement, "Why would you ever agree to that?"

"Cause I want it over with," I sighed. "I'm sick to death with the dunning calls at all hours of the day and night. I may be 'dining with Dick Humphrey' for a few months, but it will be worth it to get this fucking credit card business behind me.

"What in hell does 'dining with Dick Humphrey' mean?"

"It's an expression used in Victorian London—in the Gay 90's. It meant, 'Too poor to dine out—counting on friends to pick up the tab—eating on the cheap when broke."

"Makes as much sense as Jeanne Snow's expression 'God's Teeth!' which she uses when she's exasperated."

"I've heard you use it too—never quite knew what it meant. Anyway, when this is all over, I'm cutting up all my cards except one Visa and one Debit card and that's it—so help me—God's teeth!"

"Wrong syntax, C. Bobby. But the mention of 'God's Teeth reminds me, it's Jeanne's' birthday today. I owe her a call. He handed me his phone. "Would you mind? Look her up on my fast-dial and get her on the horn, if you can." I did and together, we sang "Happy Birthday" then handed Clive the phone, which always makes me nervous when someone is driving.

"You're not going to believe where I'm calling from, sweetheart! Nebraska. Lincoln, Nebraska to be exact. We're just passing through it, which I believe is where you were born and raised, right?" He explained in vague terms why he was making the trip and apologized for not having called her before leaving California. "Now, you'll have an excuse to visit New York," he said, not quite convincingly. "I'll email you after I get settled in. Lots of love, Jeanne. Bye, for now." He snapped the phone closed and set it in the ashtray. "I forgot to recharge it last night. The jack that fits into the cigarette lighter is in the glove compartment. Dig it out, please?"

"How you doing?" I asked, as neither of us had uttered a word for 30 miles. "I find talking out loud, if only to myself, helps me stay alert."

"I was just thinking the same thing. I can handle only so much crapola on the radio and my CDs are buried back there somewhere under the dogs."

"I have an idea. Why don't we try some good, old-fashioned conversation? I'll start by putting on my listening cap, as Mrs. Spackman, one of my Grade School teachers, used to say."

"And I'll put on my talking cap. I like that image."

"Good. I'm all ears."

"I've never told this story before—to anyone—not even Tom, but, I figure you could appreciate the residual scars." He took his eyes off the road long enough to give me a disarming, side-long glance. "You have my permission to write about it one day."

"If it's that serious, maybe you should be writing about it."

"It's serious, alright, but I can't be objective. At the end of the day—Christ, I hate that tired expression—what I mean is you're my friend—my best friend—at least for the moment and what I'm going to tell you goes a long way to explain why I have such a tough time responding to any expression of real affection."

Sensing a catch in his voice, and trying not to allow one in mine, I repeated that I was all ears.

"His name was Wayne Grace, and apparently he first saw me on TV in Toronto, in my afternoon Variety show. I was 13 and already hosting my own TV show, in case you're wondering!"

"With your talent, can't say it surprises me."

"Wayne contacted my Mom and right off, she loved his name and when he offered to become my manager, she immediately signed a contract with him—gave him full powers on the promise he'd make me a star."

"How old was this guy?"

"Late 20s—early 30s. I never knew because he never talked about his age. Anyway, when the TV show ended, Wayne brought me to New York to audition for the touring company of *Flower Drum Song*. I'd just turned 15. To save money, we shared a room at the Hotel

Lexington—had twin beds, I remember—not much bigger than cots. Anyway, it was our second night in New York, I'd finished two big auditions and Wayne felt they had gone really well. To celebrate, he treated me to supper at Tad's Steak House."

"I remember Tad's. It had red-flocked wallpaper and you could get a complete steak dinner for $1.99."

"Leave it to you to remember flocked wallpaper."

"I thought it was the height of chic at the time. But, I'm interrupting you…"

"So, we're back in the hotel room—no TV in those days, not even a radio. Wayne began to yawn a lot and started to get undressed. I noticed his voice had become husky, like he was having trouble breathing. He said he wanted to talk about something very important—so important that it couldn't be mentioned to anyone else—not my parents, not my sister and brothers, nobody." Clive shook his head, as in revulsion. "God, when I think back…Wayne said he'd become very fond of me—loved me like a brother—had my best interests at heart. Vowed he would never let any harm come to me. But for him to continue as my manager, we had to seal the deal by sleeping in the same bed—at least for part of the night. It was common thing in show-business, he assured me. Many of the biggest stars had managers who were also their boyfriends and girlfriends. You can imagine, I was taken by complete surprise—this was the last thing on my mind. I liked him well enough, but I wasn't remotely attracted to him. When he reached to unbutton my jeans, I was terrified—said something dumb like I wasn't made that way."

I sensed by his despairing tone, Clive was deep into the recollection. "He said I should think long and hard about it. Said he wasn't about to waste any more time on me without a serious commitment. There were plenty of other singers and actors and dancers who would jump at the chance to have him guide their careers and he wanted an answer that night."

"Talk about clichéd," I said. "Do all pederast-managers work from the same playbook?"

Clive shrugged. "When I refused to give him one, he began to yell at me—demanded that I 'Grow up. Be a man. Stop behaving like a kid.' I said I didn't know what he was talking about. Why would sleeping in the same bed with him make me a man? 'Then let me help you,' he said. 'I want you to leave the room *now*—'get the fuck out of here' is exactly how he put it. 'Go for a walk—clear your head—maybe think about how you're throwing away the chance of a lifetime."

"Jesus! So, what did you do?"

"What he said. Threw my stuff in my suitcase—it was an old Navy duffle-bag, actually. Went down to the lobby and sat for awhile, then left the hotel and started walking. I had no idea where I was going. I wasn't on the streets more than a few minutes when it started to rain— of course. A downpour. With no raincoat or umbrella, I ducked into the nearest doorway—I remember, it was an upscale men's shop on Madison Avenue. I stared at the mannequins and all those beautiful clothes and I started to cry. I didn't have more than a dollar and some change in my pocket—not even enough to call my family in Toronto. And what would I tell them if I did? That my manager was dumping me because I refused to let him fuck me? I could barely say the words to myself, then alone my Mom and step-Dad."

At this, he became very quiet and I could see tears forming in his eyes. "It's okay, Honeybunch," I assured him and reached to pat his shoulder. "I'm listening. You know I get it."

He wiped his nose on his sleeve. "Even after all these years, it still gets to me."

"So, then what did you do?"

"Had no choice. I went back to the room, told him I was sorry for being so selfish—yes, I actually used the word 'selfish' and endured being routinely sodomized by the son-of-a-bitch from that night on."

"God God! Didn't anybody in your family ever figure out what was going on?"

"No. The very next day I landed the part in *Flower Drum Song* and everybody was so excited and proud for me. I figured getting the part was God's reward for letting Wayne rape me—'cause that's what it was—rape."

He shook his head, like a puppy shaking off an accidental dip in the pool. "We rehearsed in New York, then moved to Detroit for the opening at the Cass, where we played for four weeks. It was the Spring of 1960. From there, the show moved to San Francisco and Los

Angeles. Since Wayne was acting as my manager *and* guardian, he was with me every minute and I had to put out for him whenever he wanted. And, before you ask, no, I didn't become some kind of vanguard for the Stockholm Syndrome."

"Never crossed my mind."

"But it does explain why I disliked getting fucked all these years, no matter how much I was turned on by somebody."

"That falls under the 'More information than I need to know' category," I chuckled, uncomfortably.

"But it does demonstrate how much I trust you," he countered.

"I appreciate that. You say you never mentioned any of this to Tom?"

"No. I was too embarrassed. Started to a couple times, but I was afraid it might piss him off so badly, he would do something terrible to Wayne."

"Is the bastard still with us?"

"Not sure. Why are you asking?"

"I'd like to meet him, ask him a few questions. Number one: 'What in the name of Christ were you thinking?' Then, depending on his answer, I might poke him in the chest and say, "There, but for the grace of God, go I."

"What, in God's teeth is that supposed to mean?"

"I don't know. It just came out."

"Well, explain yourself, Bob," he snarled, clear sign he was agitated with me.

"Now, I'm wishing I hadn't opened my mouth."

"Well, you did, Blanche—you did—and I deserve an answer. Are you saying, 'but for the grace of God' it would have been you getting the fucking or you *giving* the fucking?"

I could feel my cheeks flushing as a wave of humiliation engulfed me. "It's your story, your ugly experience and, if I'm guilty of anything, it's trying too hard to duplicate it."

"That doesn't answer my question. When you were 30, could you have demanded sex from a 15 year old kid, barely into puberty?"

"I'd be lying if I didn't admit that the *idea* might have crossed my mind, on a couple of occasions. Fortunately, my moral compass, or whatever you want to call it, kept me from acting on such urges."

"Let me get this straight. Had you been my manager back then, you would or would not have made those demands of me?"

"Jesus! Why am I suddenly on trial? Can we back up—to where I asked you whether or not this Wayne guy was still alive, and if so, where is he living now?"

"Haven't heard from him in years. Last time we spoke, he said he'd had it with the Hollywood scene—was giving it all up and retiring to Big Sur. That must have been 15 years or more. If he's still alive, he's probably growing marijuana—or dealing in cocaine—or both."

"Giving him yet another clichéd résumé. I guess what I'm trying to say—and not doing it very well, is that, given what a drop-dead beauty you were, I probably would have hit on you with equal—maybe a bit subtler fervor. But the minute you said no, I would never have risked the legal or emotional consequences. You certainly know that 'put out or get out' is not an uncommon practice in show-business, but when levied by a 30 year old man on a 15 year old boy, *that* can land you some serious jail time. I'm reminded of someone in my hometown who was sentenced to ten years in the State Pen—for fooling around with a 15 year old, despite the judge's conclusion that there was no coercion involved. Straight or gay, consensual or not, sex with minors is against the law, pure and simple."

Clive raised his hand from the wheel and held it toward my face. "Give me a minute," he said and continued to drive in silence. "Thanks for your honesty and your observations," he said, softly. "You made me think about something. Hard to believe it's something I must have been suppressing all these years."

"Listening cap still firmly in place."

"For as long as I can remember, I was told I had talent—told I could sing and dance better than Gene Kelly and Fred Astaire combined. Mom wanted me to be a star so bad, she convinced my step-Dad to give up our life in Trinidad, sell everything and move the whole family to Toronto."

"Not to be rude, but you've told me most of this before."

He nodded. "But here's the part I just realized. That night in New York, when I went back to the room and let Wayne fuck me, I rationalized it by saying to myself—and you may think this is really sick—I was doing it for Mom. I never wanted to be onstage—I mean the applause was all well and good, but the torture that preceded it—the stage fright to the point of wanting to throw up—the embarrassment of wearing lipstick and rouge—was not a fair tradeoff. Mom's dream was always at the forefront. If my becoming a star meant so much to her, and having to get fucked was the only path to getting there, then the pain and nasty hemorrhoids that followed were all out of love for her."

"I'd say, that's one helluva rationale for the books."

"And the books are where it will have to stay as it's nothing I can ever confess to her or my sister."

"I said let's try for some good, old-fashioned conversation and this one has certainly raised the bar. Has me wide awake."

"For some reason, all this talk of rape has made me hungry," Clive shrugged.

"Rape talk makes me hungry, too. Every time."

"Finally, we're in sync about something. So, let's stop for lunch?"

"Anyplace but McDonald's?" I urged. "All else will be my treat."

"Burger King? Long John Silver's? Wendy's? Taco Bell?"

"Anywhere but Burger King, Long John Silvers, Wendy's, Taco Bell or McDonald's will be my treat."

"Argh, you're tough one, Mate," Clive growled, in a half-hearted pirate's accent.

"Aye, Captain Sparrow. I saw me a sign for an Olive Garden and one for a Red Lobster, off our starboard bow."

"I vote for the Olive Garden. How bad can they screw up a bowl of pasta?"

"Pretty bad. I say Red Lobster. Never miss a chance to eat seafood in Iowa. Ranks right up there with ordering prime rib in Maine."

"New Orleans has made a total food snob out of you, hasn't it?"

"Yes, and a damned proud one, too. Besides, I hear the Jambalaya at Red Lobster could give Antoine's a run for its money."

"I wouldn't bet on it. We're in Council-fucking-Bluffs, for God sake! Looking for a quick lunch—not researching the James Beard award, so behave yourself."

"No prob. I think I just saw a helicopter from Seattle drop a crate of Dungeness crab and King Salmon right into the Red Lobster parking lot."

"Oh, Brother!" Clive rolled his eyes. "I think I'll *drop you off* in the parking lot while I find a Subway and order one of their salads."

"Relax my little Skipper. I promised to behave and I will. High time we treated ourselves to a decent meal, one with hearty paper napkins—not those puny little things they give us at KFC. I have a hankering for real salt and pepper shakers and catsup in a bottle. Remember, it's my treat."

"Good afternoon, you Guys. This here is Brittany and I'm Agnes. Brittany is the newest member of our Red Lobster family and she's gonna' be your server today." Clive took a deep breath and glared at me which translated to 'Oh, my God, a trainee—just what we need' and 'Don't you dare start, C. Robert.'

If Agnes interpreted his look, she ignored it and soldiered on. "I'll be standing by to supervise Brittany—handle any problems that should arise—though we don't expect there to be none. All part of Red Lobster quality control." With that, she gently elbowed Brittany and muttered ventriloquist-like, "Ask them what you could bring them to start."

Brittany blushed so vividly, she matched the bas relief lobster adorning the far wall. "Oh, yeah, right. What could I bring you guys to start?"

"How about a couple of menus?" I said, as benignly as I could muster.

Clive kicked me under the table. "And while you're bringing them, Brittany, I'd like to order a Bloody Bull, preferably with fresh bouillon," he said. "Tabasco and Worcestershire sauce on the side. Can you do that?"

Brittany looked to Agnes in utter panic. Agnes whispered from the side of her mouth, "Tell him you have to ask Leroy—the bartender—if he knows how to make such a thing. And ask him to repeat the name of it, again."

"Oh, Gosh. I'm sorry Sir, but I'll have to ask Leroy, the bartender, if he knows how to make…"

"I heard her," Clive snapped. "It's called a Bloody Bull—it's made like a Bloody Mary, but with beef bouillon and a little splash of tomato juice. I like to add my own Worcester and Tabasco sauce, that's why I want them on the side."

Again, Agnes leaned to Brittany. "Ask the gentleman if he has a second choice if Leroy can't make his Bloodied Bull thing." Brittany became so flustered, her hands were shaking. I glared at Clive and jumped in.

"If Leroy doesn't have the ingredients, my friend will settle for a Bloody Mary—preferably made with Smirnoff's. If not, bar vodka will do just fine. I'd like a diet 7-Up if you have it, and if you don't, I'll settle for an iced-tea. Unsweetened."

"Tell them 'thank you' and you'll be right back with their menus," Agnes hissed.

I interrupted Brittany before she could repeat it. "We don't mean to make your life difficult, dear, so just stay calm, and as soon as we get a look at the menu, we'll be ready to order, I promise."

When the two women left, I said, "And you complain about me being difficult! Could you be any more finicky? Fresh bouillon, indeed! Right up there with Gloria Swanson demanding fresh seaweed in Warren, Ohio, when she was doing "The Women" for John Kenley."

"Oh, come on. I prefer a Bloody Bull to a Bloody Mary, that's all. So did Tom."

"Quelle surprise! What do you think about Agnes? Brings supervision to a new level, I'd say."

"I was looking for the string on Brittany's back."

Miraculously, after apologizing for having to use Swanson's bouillon, Leroy produced an acceptable Bloody Bull while I endured a powdered iced tea. A quick glance at the menu and Clive announced, since I had insisted we eat here and I was paying, he was justified in ordering broiled Lobster tails and a side of onion rings. On learning Shrimp Jambalaya had been discontinued, I settled for a salmon burger, with sweet potato fries, which we mixed with the onion rings and shared. Seeing us about to finish our meal with minimal griping, the two waitresses sidled up to our table. "Ask them if they saved room for one of our delicious desserts," Agnes whispered.

"Did you save room…." Brittany began, but I cut her off.

"The answer is 'no' and you can bring me the check, Brittany." As I pulled my credit card from my wallet, I noted it was Wednesday and asked her if Iowa had a Powerball? Again, she blushed maroon and looked in panic to Agnes.

"She wouldn't know," Agnes replied. "Her faith don't permit no gambling, but I'm pretty sure there's a Lottery, 'cause the dishwashers pool their money with the cooks and play it twice a week." She turned to Brittany. "Tell them you'll be back with their receipt," which Brittany did, inaudibly.

"That poor girl's going to be a wreck by the end of the day," Clive muttered, adding, "No gambling—they must be Mormons. And what's with the Powerball, anyway?"

"I'd like to buy a ticket," I said. "I figure, if I'm ever going to win, it will be while I'm in the boonies somewhere. What better place to win an obscene amount of money than in America's Heartland?"

"Not to mention how happy the locals, sweating away at the Maytag factory, will be for you."

As if the Gods of Gambling were watching over us, the very next gas station we encountered had a banner heralding the Powerball fluttering from its price-per-gallon sign. I bought two Qwik Pics, inked both our names on each and showed them to Clive. "The Jackpot is listed at $42. million," I crowed. "If we win, we can split it."

"How thoughtful," Clive exclaimed. "After they deduct federal and state taxes, we'll each net about $85."

"That'll buy us two more tanks of gas. How bad is that?"

Just as we were about to climb into the van, a rough-looking young man appeared from behind a hedge and approached us.

"Any chance of hitchin' a ride with you guys?" he asked, exposing yellow, unkempt teeth. Before either of us could answer, he added, with a smirk, "You look like the kinda' dudes who could appreciate some company." Clive and I exchanged wary looks after which I signaled, 'Your call.'

"Depends on where you're headed," Clive responded, more politely than I would have.

"Same direction as you guys, I figure."

"And what direction is that?" I asked, trying to guess his age and whether his blue-green eyelids were the result of insomnia or eye shadow.

"East," he replied, with a crooked smile.

"Why not North or South?" I said.

"Or West?" Clive added.

"Land Rover—California plates—Malibu dealer—tells a lot."

"How so?"

"Give me a lift—I'll explain how it all works."

"Problem is, we're jam-packed," I said. "There's really no more room."

"It's a stick shift, right? I could sit between you and straddle it." He winked, "Won't be the first time I…sat on it."

If there'd been a race for eyebrow raising, Clive and I would have crossed the finish line in a dead heat. "Subtle as a train wreck," I whispered. "And where would we fit his backpack?"

"I have a special affinity for train wrecks," Clive grunted, loud enough for the stranger to hear. "I say let's give it a try. So, what's your name, Mr. Hitchhiker?"

"Monty, but my close friends call me Ty. My Mom said she named me for some old-time actor she had a crush on." He struggled out of his soiled backpack and set it on the ground beside the van.

"I'm guessing that would be Clift not Woolley," I mumbled and caught sight of Monty removing something sharp and gleaming from a side pocket.

He gestured to his backpack. "While one of you dudes figures out where to fit this, I gotta' use the crapper, but the boss-lady won't give me the key unless somebody vouches for me." Before I could caution him, Clive was accompanying Monty to the cashier's counter. "Come right back, Clive," I shouted. "I'm going to need your help." I could see through the window—some kind of altercation was taking place.

Finally, Clive and Monty emerged, brandishing the restroom key attached to a length of pipe.

"Clive, I need you over here, now," I shouted.

"What's your problem?" he growled as he crossed the lot. "If you can't find room inside, strap his backpack to the roof."

"Shut up and get in the van—now."

"What the hell's going on? What about Monty?"

"Forget him! We're splitting. I'll explain later." I started the Rover and put it in gear. "Just get in and close the damned door. You have to trust me," but he didn't budge until I revved the accelerator. "I'm not kidding, Clive. We have to get out of here, and fast." Finally, Clive leaped aboard as we careened out of the station and onto the access road. I could see Monty in the side mirror, running toward us, screaming 'Mother fuckers! Cocksuckers! I'll get you for this.' The cashier lady emerged, holding a cell phone to her ear, shouting, 'Where's my goddamned key, you little shit. I got the cops on the way.'

"He had a knife—looked like one of those fish-gutting things," I said. "Slipped it out of his backpack and took it to the men's room. God knows what he had in mind."

"You're over-reacting. Bad teeth and a fish-knife do not necessarily translate to psychotic fag killer."

"Add in a moldy backpack, filthy clothes and turquoise eye shadow and get back to me."

"Eye shadow? You sure?"

"Whether it was Revlon or Maybelline, I'm not, but the freak was wearing eye shadow."

"Maybe he was a hustler? Remember his offer to sit on the gear shift?"

"There's a Kodak moment I'll happily forgo," I sneered. "Something about his mouth—the venal look in his eyes. I'm guessing our Mon-Ty to be an ex-con."

"Not a hustler?"

"Not technically. Probably had to learn enough about it to survive in prison." After that, we lapsed into an uncomfortable silence that stretched for 10 minutes, until Clive spoke.

"I've hired guys, not as a steady diet, but every so often when I was yearning for some old-fashioned recreational sex," he confessed, punctuating the unexpected turn with his characteristic shrug. "What more convenient way to get it?"

"You're singing to the choir, my friend."

"No muss—no fuss—state clearly what you want in advance, treat them with respect and that's what you'll get back. Standing around in a bar, hoping to link up with the perfect 'lay of the day' is plain stupid."

"Choir over here."

"So, I feel like singing. Hired my first hustler when I was 25 or 26. Tom and I had had a big fight—he said it was time I started making my own life—get my own place—forgetting how many times I'd been to the pawn shop with our jewelry so we could pay the utility bills."

"You moved out of the Stone Canyon house?"

"Yep, for a time. Found a little studio apartment in, appropriately enough, Studio City. Decided to celebrate my independence by hiring a hustler."

"Nice twist on the old Emancipation Proclamation."

"I think that first guy cost 50 bucks. Of course I was nervous, but he was too. Turned out to be very sweet and a real hunk. After a rocky start, I think we both had a good time."

"And, like they say about masturbation, you don't have to look your best."

"Or make clever conversation afterwards," he added, to which we both laughed, long and hard.

"One of my favorite riddles—stop me if I've told you this already," I said. "What's the definition of eternity?"

"Sounds familiar."

"Eternity: 'After they've cum...'"

"Now I remember: After they've cum..."

"...And before they go home." We finished the answer in howling chorus.

"With you being so damned gorgeous, wasn't it intimidating for your Hired Hands?"

"Flattery will get you everything but laid, C. Bobby. But you're wrong. It's possible that my looks made it easier for the guys to deliver the deed with some enthusiasm, even if they were faking it. At least, that's what I told myself. You weren't there, so you can't challenge my theory."

"One look at you and I would have done it for free. Maybe even paid you."

"That could earn you a granola bar at the next stop, but only if I have the right change."

"Didn't any of them ever recognize you from TV?"

"One or two thought they did, but I said they must have me confused with somebody else. "Been told that before," I would say, then change the subject."

"And you got away with it?"

"Sure did. The year after I moved back in with Tom, he treated me to a couple of hustlers, just to get me out of the house. We had no shame about it."

"Tony first introduced me to the wonderful world of hustlers after we'd been dating for a year, although he hated the expression 'dating.' Our first adventure was with a scruffy type we picked up on Selma Avenue in Hollywood. Remember Selma? It was the hustler hang-out spot in Hollywood for years until the police started cracking down. Anyway, the guy must have been in his late 20's—early 30's—when we brought him home, he was so morose, kept checking his watch— Tony paid him off and we didn't repeat the escapade again."

"I think Selma Avenue may be where I found my first."

"I was so in love with Tony, I would have done it with a hedgehog, if that's what he wanted."

"There's a picture," Clive sniffed. "I never quite got what you saw in him, though, God knows, he went on to make a fortune on that Soap."

"Tony's the only one of my exes' who cut all communication with me. 'Fear of the gay,' I guess."

"Who's he kidding? Everybody in Hollywood knows his story."

"Typical Jack-Mormon. The Book of Mormon teaches them to feel guilty about anything pleasurable that doesn't generate more Mormons."

"I heard it was the same with Jews until Harvey Fierstein came along."

"Your revelation that Tom treated you to a couple of hustlers doesn't come as a big surprise to me."

"Does anything—ever?"

"I recall seeing him at Numbers Bar one night—guessing it was in the late 80's. Seated by himself in a booth, obviously liquored up, glaring about the room, and when I said hello, he hissed, all but spit at me. It was very upsetting at the time."

"The late 80's," Clive nodded. "That was the second period of his artistic and emotional nadir."

"Really? I could never figure whether his reaction was over being recognized in such a compromising place or fear I'd report it to you, or because he was snockered, or maybe all three."

"Shortly after that he joined AA. Said it did him a world of good, but he never trusted the 'anonymous' part. He always suspected there were informants from the tabloids working the room."

"Informants can be alcoholics, too."

"Why didn't I think of that?" Clive grumbled. "Hi, I'm Sidney and I'm spying for the National Enquirer," he lisped.

"Hi, Sidney," I answered. "Welcome to AA. If you don't mind sharing—how much does the Enquirer pay you for spying on us?"

"God grant me the serenity to accept the things I cannot change and the courage to smack this man silly," Clive said—to which we giggled and high-fived each other.

"I don't think I ever told you," I said, "but I met Robby, my office manager, at Numbers. Wasn't long after our first assignation, he came to work for me."

"I always thought there was something a bit devious—my polite word for crooked—about Robby."

"Your intuition was right, but that's blood long under the bridge. Blood we don't need to suction up at this juncture. Robby was very good looking and remarkably versatile in the sack. I was aware he augmented his income with other after hour 'consultations.' I never asked who else he was seeing, just always played it safe."

"Only one time I heard about somebody getting ripped off by a hustler," Clive mused. "It was Garth Winthrop—the florist? Claimed he had some expensive jewelry stolen by an Argentinean hustler. Factor in that Garth was a boozer and mean as a snake when he was drunk."

"Moral," I interjected. "Never leave the Cartiers and Omegas lying around."

"Or digital cameras. That's the only thing I ever had stolen. Then again, it's possible I misplaced it."

"Or gave it away. From what I've seen, you've always been Mr. Too Generous."

"Thank you for noticing," he smiled. "You're determined to earn that Granola bar."

"Yes, and think about what we just extemporized. It could be an absolute ratings grabber for our appearance on Oprah."

"And, if Oprah thinks the topic is too tawdry for her housewives," he teased, "Regis would gladly pick up the slack."

"You may have told me but, I've forgotten, Clive. The reason you gave up California and moved to Florida was...?"

"Probably sounds a bit corny now, but after Tom died, so much of my life went with him. I was truly on my own for the first time. I wanted to experience what it was like to start life over, leave all the bad stuff behind me."

"Escaping to a safer environment, as it were."

"If that didn't sound so damned Scientologese, I'd say yes—I was escaping."

"Nobody could blame you for it. I, for one, envied the idea."

"In a way, I was copying you. You ran away to Hawaii back in the 70's and look at the great success you had?"

"Thank you, but comparing Hawaii to Florida is mixing pineapples and oranges. You couldn't pay me to live in Florida."

"Apparently most of my friends felt the same way. I was there six months before anyone came to visit me. And then, only after I'd paid for their plane ticket."

"I rest my case. Didn't your Mother come to live with you, after awhile?"

"Briefly," he nodded. "But being her favorite son, you can guess what that meant. 'I'll be your housekeeper—your private secretary—save you a fortune,' she said. 'I'll take care of the dogs when you're away. You'll hardly notice I'm around.' 'Yeah, right Mom.' To keep the peace *and* my sanity, I bought her a little house nearby and moved her in."

"I remember, one time you asked me to call her on her Birthday. I reminded her we're both Sagittarians, which she got a kick out of. She sounded so happy being there—close to you." I winked at him. "You're a good son, Clive."

"Would you mind telling that to my creditors? Anyway, it wasn't long after my Florida move when Rick died."

"He was in LA at the time?"

"No. We had split shortly before Tom passed and Rick moved back to Tucson. We stayed good friends—talked on the phone fairly regularly. He was teaching dance at a friend's studio, which he loved."

"From AIDS, right?"

"Yes. Unfortunately his doctors put him on the cocktail too late. Had he started earlier, it might have saved him."

"So sad. Such a beautiful guy."

"I think it was Rick's death that confirmed I'd made the right decision to leave California behind me and start afresh."

"What a rough time it must have been for you. But on the upside, between the two houses in Ft. Lauderdale and the retreat in the Bahamas, you were able to invest some serious capital in real estate."

"Don't remind me. I always seemed to sell too soon or too late after the market crested." He shrugged. "Probably the main reason I'm in the present mess."

"Wasn't long after you moved to Ft. Lauderdale, you took up pilot training, if I remember correctly. Whatever happened with that?"

"I took classes for a couple of months. Loved it, at first. Thought I might even find a new career as a pilot."

"I remember—you were so excited—looking forward to your first solo flight."

"Yeah, and I finally got to do it. Quite a thrill. Gave my self confidence a big lift—small pun intended."

"Then you stopped. Care to say why?" I detected a flicker of annoyance in his eyes before he responded.

"The training was expensive—about to become more so. And it involved a helluva lot more homework than I bargained for. My fantasy of graduating from a single-engine Cessna to a Boeing 727 evaporated the night I worked 'til dawn trying to analyze a Caribbean weather chart."

"You must have known weather was going to be a big part of the training?"

"Of course I did. But truthfully it wasn't just that. One afternoon, I overheard a couple of instructors talking about how impossible it was for anyone over 30 to break into the piloting game, unless they had prior experience in the military. I was already in my 40's—I've never been in the military and never piloted anything bigger than my Porsch coupe. Based on their conversation, I figured there wasn't much hope for me."

"So, you never went on to get your license?"

"No, and I don't have any real regrets about it. I had the thrill of taking the plane up solo, flying around for half and hour and landing it. I can honestly say, enough of my fantasy had been fulfilled."

"Very mature thinking, Clive. I've had my Icarus-wings singed enough times to know—not every fantasy has to become a reality, to find true happiness."

"*Icarus-wings singed*—what a whimsical expression! Sort of a softball version of what Tom always said, '*You never get it all*.'"

"But it sure is fun trying," I countered, not intending to have the last word.

"Tom was never much for warm and fuzzy homilies."

"Tell me about it. I'll never forget one of the first conversations he and I ever had—not long after I started coming to the Stone Canyon house to rehearse with you. Out of nowhere, he asked me, 'What is your sign?' When I told him 'Sagittarius,' he said, 'And how old are you?' '32.' After a pregnant pause, he said, 'I'm surprised you're not more successful by now.' Put me on the defensive for weeks, I can tell you."

"If it's any comfort, he eventually concluded you were a 'late bloomer' and said as much after we visited you in Hawaii and again in New Orleans."

"Never too late to hear a compliment. I'll file it under *posthumous approval.*"

"We've been gone for four days, and I haven't heard you call your Mother once."

"Because I don't have anything to say to her right now. It can wait until we get to the city."

"Two things that make Mothers nervous—calling with bad news or not calling with any news. Anyway, you heard me promise Eva I'd make every effort."

"And you have. Now give it a rest."

Source: hospitality-on.com

Motel 6, Des Moines, IA—West #1408
7655 Office Plaza Drive North
I-80 at 74th Street, Exit #121
West Des Moines, IA, 50266 Phone: (515) 267-8885

Day Five

Thursday, May 19th—Des Moines, IA to

Minutes after checking out of the motel, we were lost trying to leave town. Road construction seemed to be going on at every junction and poorly marked detour signs had us circling Des Moines twice, which made for a tense morning. Eventually, with the help of two maps and the Rover's compass, we found our way to Hwy #80 eastbound.

"Did you ever want children?" I asked, looking to shift attention away from my inchoate map reading.

"Now, who's being oblique?"

"Touché. But did you?"

"A couple of years before we met, Tom adopted a boy through the Foster Parents Plan. The kid's name was Pietro—an Italian orphan who lived with an older brother in Rome, but Tom never mentioned anything about it to me. I only learned about it after reading an interview he gave to the LA Times."

"Did you ever meet the boy?"

"No, nor did Tom ever encourage it. I'm pretty sure he continued to support Pietro until he came of age—even when Tom was experiencing some rough patches financially. The Times article said the kid was 13 at the time, so, if he's still with us, he'd be in his late 40's by now. Odd how, all these years, I've never thought anything about him until you brought it up."

"Ever had the desire to sire one of your own?"

"No way. One time, Tom and I talked about donating our sperm to a surrogate Mother, but nothing came of it. All our animals were adopted from shelters or the SPCA. They were children enough for us."

"I entertained the idea of adopting with Barry," I confessed. "Ever so briefly. More in an effort to hold our relationship together than actually wanting to be a parent."

"Thank God you didn't follow through."

"Amen! I have Barry to thank for that. I've resisted parenthood for many reasons; firstly, my restless nature; secondly, fear that I'd be lavishing them with gifts at lunchtime and banishing them to the attic with bread and water at suppertime."

"Is there a thirdly?"

"Yeah. How could I handle it if a child of mine turned out to be physically or mentally handicapped? Or worse, a Republican?"

"And the Self Awareness Award goes to...? Clive flipped down the visor and addressed the mirror. "Envelope, please? The winner is C. R. Holloway, who, despite his gut-wrenching confession, hasn't lived anyplace with an attic since he was 12 years old."

"You never told me how you and Tom first met. Any particular reason?"

"Maybe I'm saving it for my memoirs."

"Which manuscript I hereby offer to proof. Why not a little preview? I find a verbal discourse often helps structure the printed word."

"Or by repeating it to fools, reduces the subject to small beer," Clive sniffed.

"Love that expression, but since I don't drink beer and I'm no fool, it doesn't apply to me."

"Does anything—ever?"

"Yes. Like my sincere desire to encourage a multi-talented friend to stretch his autobiographical wings."

"Holloway, if persuasion could be bottled, you'd be..."

"...a millionaire. How many times have I heard that? In contrast to my Mother's insistence that I had a champagne appetite on a beer budget and my eyes were always bigger than my belly."

"She can't say that about your belly, now."

"Good one. Very Don Rickles. How do you do it, Clive?"

"You bring out the best in me, C. Bob."

"If that's true, then give it up, Honeybunch. Tell us how you and Tom first met?

He rolled his eyes and sighed. "It was 1963, I think—my first or second day at Universal, rehearsing the part of the singing delivery boy in "Send Me No Flowers" with Doris Day. Mother was beside herself when she heard Rock Hudson and Tony Randall were also in it. "My son is going to be a star!" she said to everyone at St. John's Hospital, where she was working as Head Housekeeper."

"So where did you meet? In the parking lot? On a sound stage? Make-up trailer? I'm crazy for locational details."

"It was in the Studio Commissary—don't really remember who saw who first—maybe it happened simultaneously—that was always Tom's take on it. But, as the saying goes, hindsight provides the more romantic memory. Bells, chimes, sirens and fireworks went off. At least in my head."

"How did you manage to signal each other—given the oppressive times and your age difference?"

"Not exactly sure. I think Tom wrote his number on a napkin and slipped it to Wayne, my manager."

"Isn't that special! From what you described, that would have put Wayne on high alert. Needing to guard his steady piece and all."

"Only you would refer to me as a 'steady piece.' Don't know whether to feel flattered or insulted."

"Try both—it's good exercise for flexibility. So what was Wayne's reaction?"

"He was such a Sammy Glick—never showed anything but pleasure that we'd connected with someone famous or about to be."

"So, what happened next? You can't leave me dangling."

"Who says I can't? Like Tom always said, 'You never get it all.' That's as much of the story as I care to remember and therefore that's as much as you're going to get, for now."

"Unfair! Just when your story was getting really, really...boring."

"Au contraire, C. Bobby. Shows I know when to edit. When to hold back—leave something to the listener's imagination. Unlike some..."

"Don't start!" I interrupted. "Your superior attitude can come across as meaner than a snake."

"It's too early in the day for that sort of accusation."

"Is it? I remember one morning on Maui, vacationing with you and your sister, after my first big show had opened at the Monarch Room, with my sets and lighting—to rave reviews, I might add. I finally lost it and snapped back after your constant derision of me, which you never hesitated to do, even in public, *despite* my being the one footing the bill for the entire trip."

"You always oversell everything. Be it a movie or a play, the menu in a restaurant, the decor in somebody's house. When you like something, C. Bobby, you go overboard. After awhile it makes people distrust you."

"We've been down this road how many times before, Clive? We're polar opposites on this point. I figure, what I lack in talent I make up for by sharing my enthusiasm with the world. Life is still a big adventure for me. Carving out a career in the arts, without a formal education, has been my life-long pursuit—continues to be, if truth be told."

"Mine too, but you've been known to wax for 20 minutes about a ham sandwich. 'You *have* to try it,' you say. 'It's the best ham sandwich in town, the rye bread is extra crunchy, the mustard is out of this world, and the pickles are from God's own barrel.' It can be amusing the first couple of times, but what's the point in raving on and on like that?"

"I don't think of it as 'raving on.' Complimenting someone on their work, when I truly mean it, has paid off in spades and fostered several unique friendships, throughout my life. Present company—no exception."

"Compliment as diplomatic de-fuser. Shrewd and deftly done, C. Rob."

"You're welcome. And while we're waxing serious, I have another topic I've been meaning to talk to you about."

"Should I be wearing my lead underwear?"

"Metaphorically, you're not too far off. The subject is AIDS."

"Thank God it's nothing serious this close to lunch."

"Thought about it a hundred times over the last few years. I'm just damned lucky. As the saying goes—'There but for the grace of God...'"

"Makes two of us," Clive nodded. "By the mid-90's, after Tom died—I gave up counting how many friends I'd lost."

"Same here. Seemed like I was going to a funeral or a memorial every other week."

"I finally stopped going, altogether," Clive admitted. "Couldn't shed another tear or listen to another eulogy about a life cut short in its prime."

"Ever wondered why neither of us contracted it?" I asked.

"Assume it was by using condoms and being very careful if you were a bottom."

"Which I stopped being a long time ago. After the anal cyst surgeries—I suffered through three of them over the years—the doctors said it was a condition I'd likely inherited from my Dad—not the result of anal sex, but I wasn't about to take any chances."

"Also, the risks of being an unprotected top were so inconclusive—why gamble with it?" he shrugged. "Shut up and put on the damned rubbers."

"Hate the things," I confessed. "Between having to wear a condom and a wank, I'll take the wank, any day."

"I wouldn't go that far," Clive snickered.

"AIDS was never mentioned in any of Tom's obituaries. In truth, isn't that what he died of? It was certainly the rumor, all over town."

"No, he didn't and it pisses me off that that rumor is still being bandied about. His doctor's certified his death was due to stomach cancer. He *was* HIV positive, but the official cause of his death was stomach cancer."

"Can't stomach cancer be the result of AIDS?"

Clive was becoming agitated. "I'm sure it can, but Tom didn't want his readers or his relatives to know, especially his brother."

"Seems so weird. Even after the revelation of Rock Hudson and Tony Richardson and how many other big names?

"He was adamant about keeping it quiet."

"On his death bed? He still wanted to stay in the closet on his deathbed?"

"From your tone, I think we'd best change the subject."

"Okay, but I see it as Tom's selfish silence helped the Dark Ages continue into the millennium."

"That's mean-spirited, hyperbolic, judgmental bullshit. So typical of you, Bob. Why would you want to say such a hateful thing?"

"I didn't say it to be hateful. It's just that I'm constantly appalled at the pain and destruction that's fomented by famous men staying in the closet."

"And that gives you license to make such a sweeping judgment about Tom?"

"Notice that you just called me Bob. Exactly like he used to, no matter how many times I asked him to call me Robert or C. Robert."

"He thought C. Robert was pretentious. And, after this conversation, I'm thinking he was right."

There's something about a long road trip that dulls one's sense of time—at least it does mine. I think nothing's been said for half-an-hour when it's actually been less than ten minutes. And, when the words are angry, even less real time has actually passed. As if to break the ice, there appeared a series of billboards heralding the Lavender Crest Winery, outside Colona, IL. "Who knew Illinois had a wine industry?" I offered, cautiously.

"And one sitting on a crest of lavender?" Clive added, with a smirk. "Very Laura Ashley. What the hell is a lavender crest, anyway?"

"The sign says they serve lunch. Let's find out."

"It's way out of our way, C. Bobby. I'm not that curious."

"Come on. Where's your sense of adventure? Anybody can say they've been to a winery in the Napa Valley. How many people do you know who've been to a winery in Colona, Illinois?"

"No one. Nor do I know anyone who's ever been to Illinois."

"There you go," I assured him. "Now, you'll be able to say you know two people."

"Hardly wait to add that to my résumé. Besides, I don't drink wine."

"But you love fresh squeezed juice. Maybe they make one with lavender."

"Incorrigible!"

Source: www.lavendercrest.com

Our lunch area features a variety of drinks, wraps, paninis, sandwiches, soup, pastries and other delicacies.

Within minutes we pulled into the parking lot, which was nearly vacant, save for a couple of vehicles. The Winery's main entrance opened directly into its gift shop, where a pouter-breasted matron stood by the cash register inside an immaculately appointed kiosk. When told we were looking for lunch, the woman cheerfully handed us the single sheet menu and instructed us to place our order with her. After asking myriad questions, Clive ordered an avocado and radicchio wrap, which came with a fruit cup and white grape juice. I ordered a turkey and goat cheese Panini and a lemonade. The kindly lady directed us to the dining area, "Just past the Banquet Hall and Tasting Room you'll find our al fresco café," she cooed. "Not to worry, it's covered by a brand new awning. Our local guests love it. They say it reminds them of Rome or Paris."

"How neat is this?" I said, gesturing to the prefabed gazebo perched atop a nearby knoll. "Squint and you're in Rome."

"Doesn't take much to make you happy," Clive carped.

"Your order will be here any minute," the matron assured us. "Oh, and if you'd like, you may keep your menus as a souvenir," she added, as she backed through the doorway.

"You have to admit, it beats the hell out of a McDonald's," I said, unnecessarily."

He shrugged. "We'll see after we've tasted the food."

"What's with the Mr. Grumpy act? Frowning is unbecoming to anyone as good-looking as you. Makes for permanent wrinkles."

"You're right. It's just that, the closer we get to the city, the more I'm thinking about the mountain of shit I have to confront."

"I know, my friend. But I also know how 'Being in the moment' can work miracles. Look at those rolling hills—row after row of neatly staked grape vines. We could be in Tuscany." With that, the food arrived and delighted us with its presentation and portions, making it easy to forgive its bland taste and heartening me to reveal another long-held secret. "The other day, your story about Chuck Connors and the *Cowboy in Africa* debacle triggered a memory for me—something I've never told you. Now seems like good time as any to get it off my chest."

"When did this become 'Clive's Cross-Country Confessional?'"

"The day you asked me to accompany you on this trip. Now, may I continue, Father?"

"After you've placed an appropriate tithing in the collection plate."

"And what is considered an appropriate tithing?"

"Twenty bucks gets you into the booth."

"Sorry, I only carry big bills. Can you break a fifty?"

"No. But we'll put the difference towards the next fill-up. Now, get on with it, while I finish my grape juice and decide how many Hail Marys I'm going to give you."

"You remember how we met—when I took over the direction of *Park*?"

"With less than two weeks to go before opening night. How could I forget?"

"Julienne Marie was playing your sister—she quit and had to be replaced ASAP. I held auditions in the early mornings while we continued to rehearse around her character. God, this is hard…"

"I'm not sure where you're headed, but it doesn't sound like a Praise Jesus moment."

"It could be, if you'd let me get through it, Your Grace."

"Proceed, my son."

"From the get go, it was obvious you were very talented, no question. But I felt you were way too good looking and sophisticated to be playing the tortured son in that blue-collar family. I told Albert McLeary that I wanted to replace you while there was still time. He was adamantly against it and assured me that you were a dedicated pro—that you took direction well. Reluctantly, and under enormous pressure, I agreed to find a way to make it work—which I did to decidedly mixed results, as the critics were unanimous in pointing out."

Clive was very quiet for some moments. "And this relates to the debacle with Connors, how?"

"At the *Park* opening night party, I learned how close Tom and McLeary were. Tom had starred in several of Albert's NBC *Matinee Theatre* adaptations. I figured that explained how you came to be cast."

"Not quite, though it's true, I never auditioned for the part. Albert had just seen me in a production of *Seventeen* at the Pasadena Playhouse."

"Right. And Albert must have been aware of Connors' cruelty and was determined to protect you. No way was he going to allow me or anyone to replace you."

"Albert was the last of the true gentlemen," Clive responded, quietly.

"In the ensuing years, I've often shuddered to think what would have happened if he had. We'd never have become friends—maybe never even seen each other again, and if we had, never spoken. We have Albert McLeary's rapport with Tom and his concern for your well being to thank for our friendship."

"You could have let me go to my grave without sharing that back story."

"No, I couldn't. Our honest friendship is too valuable to me."

"And still, you wonder why I never became a star?" he sighed. "Can we change the subject now?" He handed me his glass. "Taste this and tell me which part of Tuscany we're in."

"The magical part. I look at all those vines and trellises and see merry Munchkin mercenaries marching on Oz."

"Good God! Sounds like I should have ordered the lemonade."

Back on the road—me at the wheel, Clive said, "It's your turn to tell a funny story."

"What for? Mine are so dull, compared to yours. 'Theatre wannabe comes to New York fresh out of high school, works his ass off for decades and eventually 'claws his way to the middle'—which I'm thinking might make a great title for *my* autobiography."

"Your Blanche Yurka story, for instance. Tom loved it and used to tell it, *occasionally* giving you credit. But nobody tells it better than you, C. Bobby."

"If you insist: I'd been taking private acting classes from Yurka for several weeks, when she called to say she was leaving town to appear in *I Remember Mama* at the Cleveland Playhouse—and asked me to ride along in the taxi to Grand Central to help with her bags. Once we settled in the back seat, she spoke to me in her practical, housefrau voice: 'While I'm away, Robert, I want you to work on Hamlet's speech to the Players and Mark Anthony's eulogy to Julius Caesar and...Oh dear God! The cabbie's taken a wrong turn! It'll cost us a fortune!' She rapped on the plexi-panel and shifted to her imperious, Shakespearean voice: 'Drivah, do you think you could negotiate a U turn heah? Ah, there's a good man! We thank you.' Then, back to me, flat, practical, "Now, Robert, you also need to be looking at Marchbanks in Candida, Act Two. Can you remember all that, dear? Shouldn't you be writing it down?"

Clive laughed aloud. "Must be where you picked up your piss-elegant accent."

"Now who's the pot calling the kettle beige," I replied. "Always thought 'Clive Clerk' sounded a bit cutesy, like it was a made-up stage name."

"You weren't alone. Lots of people did—even I came to think it. Of course it wasn't. When Mom divorced our real Father and married James Clerk, he legally adopted all of us. Fortunately, we loved James from day one. Even you once said you thought he was the kindest, gentlest man you'd ever met."

"That I did and, second to my Daddy, he was. What confused me on first meeting was that none of you looked a thing like James."

"Mom used to say, behind James' back of course, we should be grateful."

"Hilarious. That's exactly what my sister and I say about Harry, our Mother's boyfriend."

"After James died—bear in mind, he had been the only father we ever knew for most of our lives—I thought the time was right to change my name back to Wilson."

"How did you accomplish it?"

"Involved petitioning the courts in Trinidad, Canada and the US. Having duel citizenship made it even more complicated—took an army of lawyers, but I was finally able to restore my name to Wilson."

"So, technically, your name is Clive Reginald Clerk-Wilson?"

"As Kitty Carlisle used to say, 'Isn't he clevah?' Anyway, after it was all official, Doe and I travelled to England for a reunion with our real Father, which was an interesting experience, if a bit surreal."

"Ever thought of hyphenating the two family names?"

He shook his head. "Sounds pretentious, but leave it to you to suggest it."

"Pretensions R Us—and since the Brits pronounce Clerk as Clark, think how much fun it would be to say, 'I'd like to introduce you to my friend, Clive Clark-Wilson?"

"Fun for whom? Is there no end to your riffs?"

"No, especially after a good lunch. Shall we move on to your camp nick-name? How did that come about?"

"Who said I had one?"

"I overheard it at a party, years ago. Somebody referred to you as *Clara*, and I had to ask who they were talking about."

"Must have been Trent. He's the only one who would call me that in public."

"I think it was. So, *how did it* come to be?"

"Trent and I were roommates, on and off, for years. Whenever Tom and I had a fight or he had relatives coming to visit, or there was a columnist looking to do an 'at home' story, I had to go into hiding—forego being 'Tryon's Boy Toy 'til things cooled down."

"What an era. Still, Clara's an awfully campy name. Strikes me as more than a bit fey for you."

"I didn't mind, really—long as it was among close friends. Remember, I was still Clive Clerk and hadn't thought about changing my name yet. Trent and I were doing the dishes one night. I dropped one of his Mother's crystal glasses and broke it. He called me a 'clutz,' then tacked on 'Clara.' Wasn't long before it became 'Clara Clutz, and eventually, 'Clara Clerk, the Clutz.' Like you, Trent loves euphony, so it stuck. Now you satisfied?"

"I've never been comfortable with the tradition of Gay men referring to each other as 'girlfriend' and 'sister.' Consequently, I could never imagine calling you 'Clara.' Nor did I ever, even during those stretches when we weren't speaking. I've always had too much respect for you."

"That's nice to hear. But, knowing you, there's more, right?"

I glanced at him, once again dazzled by his classically chiseled features and extraordinary complexion. "Ultimate confession time," I said. "May strike you as a bit redundant, but hear me out."

"I think I have some idea where this is headed."

"Okay, but here goes anyway: Shortly after we first met, there were weeks—months even, I was so obsessed with you I couldn't sleep. So I came up with the idea of creating the nightclub act, partially as an excuse to spend time with you on an every-other-evening basis. I even talked Jerry Powell, my accompanist friend, into volunteering his time and talent on the project.

"Yes and despite my gut feeling, I went along with it and the three of us managed to do some damned fine work. Proof is on that demo tape we made. I hope you saved the master?"

"In my files, somewhere," I replied. "Haven't listened to it in years."

"I'd love to have a copy, when you get around to it."

"Anyway, all through that time, I kept wondering 'Why can't he throw me a small bone? Something—anything to indicate he recognizes the depth of my infatuation?"

"Maybe I was too used to it. People fawning over me, I mean. Maybe I valued you too much as a friend to risk spoiling our friendship. With you, like so many others, I was afraid the slightest encouragement would be misinterpreted—an extended hug might give you the idea I was ready to go all the way."

"And you never were?"

"With you, no. Not in the least—sorry to report."

"Jesus, that's tough. You knew all along and yet you never gave me the slightest indication you were aware of my true feelings for you?"

"You may think what I'm going to say sounds like something from Jane Austin, or I'm the vainest person you've ever known, but here it is: Having great beauty can be a terrible burden. Tom used to say it all the time. Great beauty freights an awful responsibility."

"Freights? Tom used the word freights in that context?'

"Tom was a genius with words, don't forget."

"How could I?"

"And I'm no slouch."

"In case I hadn't noticed. Come to think about it, there's something else I never told you. It might support Tom's theory. Unfortunately, the only way to tell it is to tell the whole thing."

"Do your best to edit it down to a half-hour," he joked.

"I think it was that time you and Tom were vacationing at the Royal Hawaiian. Apparently there'd been a big upset between you two—it was a rainy Sunday morning—God knows why I remember that detail—but you came looking for me—took a taxi from Waikiki to the Opera scene shop, but I was elsewhere. Richard Gullicksen was Honolulu Opera's resident scenic designer and a major closet case, consequently overly-protective of his teen-aged son. His name was Stefan, and he worked on set construction with Richard.

Ironic coincidence: we were mounting Menotti's *The Last Savage*, which could be the perfect sub-title for this story. Apparently Stefan met you at the door and had an immediate and totally freaky reaction to you. An hour or so later, Richard pulled me aside from a lighting rehearsal in the Opera House and read the riot act to me.

"Why in the world would you let someone like that near my scene shop?" he thundered.

"What in the name of Christ are you talking about?" I responded.

"I'm talking about that friend of yours. The one who came to the shop this morning, looking for you."

"That would be Clive. And, the problem is?"

"Stefan was in shock. 'What's Holloway doing associated with a guy like that?' he asked me. "Pretty enough to be a girl. And so effeminate! If that guy really is Holloway's friend, I've lost all respect for him."

"I don't know what in hell you and Stefan are talking about," I fired back. "Clive is very good looking, to be sure, but if anything, he's the antithesis of effeminate."

"Not according to Stefan. And my son is very savvy about these things—and he never lies," Richard raged.

"Let me get this right," I said. "Your son greets a handsome man at the scene shop door—immediately goes into high upset—and complains to his Daddy? Forgive me, but I find that totally insane."

"I caught a glimpse of him," Richard said, "and I have to agree with Stefan."

At that point, I was so rattled, my hands were shaking. It took me a moment or two to summon a reply. "Forgive me, Richard, but this is sounding like 'the Lady doth protest too much.' In this case, it might even be the plural."

Richard raised his fist to my face. "You faggots are all alike. Covering for each other. I ought to punch you out—maybe teach you a lesson you won't forget."

At that moment, the Stage Manager happened by and stepped between us. "Easy there, Gentlemen. I don't know what's going here, but this is not the time or place for a fight." Simultaneously, Gian Carlo Menotti, who was directing his rarely produced work, walked up to me. "Signore Holloway, I'm ready to begin. Your border lights are hanging too low. I hate seeing the lights. Come, we re-trim them together."

Richard, purple with rage, greeted Menotti with an obsequious bow and 'Buon jorno, Maestro,' then raced to the men's room. Somehow I managed to get through the rehearsal. Later, when I tried to speak with Richard, he wouldn't hear of it. That nasty exchange sullied our relationship ever after."

"Believe it or not," Clive whispered, "I don't remember anything about that day except a vague recollection of having an argument with Tom—which wasn't unusual, whenever we vacationed together."

"As if Karma needed further vindication, Richard made the Police Report in the Honolulu papers some years later, after being badly beaten in a men's room in Kailua."

"Appreciate your defending me, but I can't help wondering why you waited so long to tell me this crappy story?"

"Couldn't bring myself to report it at the time. But now, after hearing Tom's theory, I thought it might help to confirm it. By simply showing up, great beauty can cause disturbing reactions."

Clive pondered my answer for a few moments. "So where is Gullicksen now?"

"He died in 2003. The obituaries were full of compliments for his work—entirely justified—he was very talented. Naturally, they avoided any mention of his trashy exploits."

"And his son?"

"Last I heard, he was living in California. But, that bizarre experience stuck with me all these years. I've had no reason to contact him."

"I can barely process it now. Can't imagine how I would have handled it then."

"But it does ratify Tom's theory. We ugly peasants, working in the coal mines and sweat shops, are fond of saying, 'Beauty may only be skin deep, but give me some of that skin.'"

Clive glanced at the gas gauge. "Think we'll be okay for another half hour. Can we move onto something else? Like ten minutes of peace and quiet? Surely we've exhausted this subject?"

"Not quite. I need to set something emphatically straight. You mean to tell me that, despite knowing how infatuated with you I was, you never even thought about offering me so much as a hand job?"

"That's disgusting. Now, you've gone too far, Bob."

"Disgusting? To whom? When did you take the vows of verbal chastity?"

"You know what I mean. The fine line between love and lust is easily crossed."

"You mean like that morning in the Honolulu Hotel, when you took the red-eye from LA and pretended to surprise me? Said it was because you missed me so much? Within fifteen minutes I went from rejoicing to abject rejection, overhearing you masturbate in the shower. After you dried off, you came over and kissed me on the cheek, told me how much I meant to you and confessed you were there to escape the humiliation of Tom's infidelities."

"My, my. After all this time! The way you tell it makes it sound more hurtful than it probably was."

"Trust me, it was hurtful. Profoundly hurtful, as only a Beauty Freighter could inflict it! And with its brave recounting, I take Match Point."

"Match point! You don't know the first thing about tennis."

"True, but I know I've struck some kind of nerve when you get all red-faced and that vein in your temple starts pulsating."

"Oh you do, do you?" After an extended silence, he cooed, "I wonder what little Bobby's Mother would have to say about this conversation?"

"She wouldn't understand a word of it!" I held up my cell phone. "If you don't believe me, ask her yourself."

"As usual, you're going too far."

"Too far! You're the one that dragged my Mother into the conversation—to avoid confronting anything close to the bone—or maybe I should say 'boner,' small pun intended."

"That's even more disgusting. I've a mind to turn on the radio. The AM radio. Maybe find a sermon on the evils of self-abuse."

"Or the joys. For that, you'll have to switch to FM."

"They don't call you 'Last Word Holloway' for nothing."

"I do think my Mother would wonder why you'd been so mean to her son when all he was attempting to do was offer you his unconditional love."

"Unconditional love! Give me a break! If your Mother taught you that unconditional love included an obligatory wank, is it any wonder you're so fucked up?"

"Eventually, I did get over you. Right after you left Honolulu, that first time; I had an auditing session with Roger Taylor—an old friend from St. Hill days. Very sympathetic, very capable auditor. I remember confessing that I was obsessed with you—that I was having trouble functioning on the most basic level—because you didn't return my feelings in any way that I could find satisfaction. In the session, I remember having a vivid image of standing on some kind of disc-shaped platform in space, just me and a joy stick flying around the universe. Hubbard called that kind of recall 'Space Opera,' which pretty well describes it. When I came back from what must have been a very deep trance, I felt so much lighter—the weight of the universe had magically lifted from my shoulders. What the hell roaring around the heavens on an 8' diameter surfboard had to do with erasing the pain of my unrequited love for you, I haven't the slightest. But it worked. And it lasted—mostly—or I wouldn't be here now."

"I'm happy for you. Happy for both of us, actually," Clive whispered.

"How many miles is it from Des Moines to Hammond, Indiana?"

"MapQuest says it's only 341," I replied. "But it feels like we've been driving a helluva lot longer than that."

"We have. The odometer says we clocked over 475 miles today."

"Probably logged 50 of them trying to get out of Des Moines."

"And another 50 driving to that goofy winery in Illinois," Clive countered.

"Well, what do you say? Hammond's just ahead. Shall we call it a day?"

"It'll make it our shortest," he declared, "but I'm exhausted."

Source: www.motel6.com

Motel 6 Hammond—#692
3840 179th Street
I-80/94 at Cline Avenue/SR 912, Exit #5
Hammond, IN, 46324
Phone: (219) 845-0330

Motel 6 Policies:
Check-in age is 21 years or older. In collaboration with local authorities, this specific location requires a photocopy of guest identification upon check-in.

For a mere $2.99, Motel #692 offered WiFi service. After our sumptuous repast at Wendy's, I was able to catch up on a small avalanche of emails. Eventually, I thought to log onto the Iowa Lottery website and check the results for Wednesday evening.

"Damn! You're not going to believe this, Clive—but we didn't have even one of the winning numbers on our Lottery tickets."

"Thank God!" he sighed. "Now, I can call the workers at the Maytag factory and tell them to put down their rakes and torches."

Day Six

Friday, May 20th—Hammond, IN to

Friday was the worst. It seemed the further East we drove, the more detours we encountered. On leaving Hammond, we made a wrong turn and missed the onramp to Highway 80 completely. Stubbornly soldiering on, it was nearly two hours before we were forced to stop for gas and ask directions.

"You're in Michigan" said the smirking station owner. "If you Boys left Hammond bound for Ohio, you done backtracked." His revelation amused him so, it provoked a salvo of porcine snorts. "Goofed pretty bad, I'd say. You Boys are a good 90 mile from where you need to be headed."

"Ah have no idee what we done wrong, Sir," I said, in my gravelliest country voice, "But if you could point out on this here map how to git us back onta Highway 80 headed East, we'd be mighty obliged." Clive shot me a look that said, 'What in God's teeth provoked that shit-kicking accent?' I lowered my head and raised my brow to indicate he should say nothing.

The owner studied our license plates. "California. Yer a mighty long way from home, Boys." He peered into the back window of the Rover. "Cain't be very comfortable up there for them cockers—'specially since they look to be pure-breds."

Clive said, "They're doing just fine, Sir. My girls love car rides. They've made this trip several times."

"My wife and me—jus' lost our little cocker back in April. Name was Wabash. Had her twelve years. 'Bout broke our hearts."

"Sorry to hear that…" I spotted his name tag. "Mr. Furr. Real sorry, but if you could mark on our map…?"

"Them dogs are jus' what Minnie an' me been lookin' all over fer. Tell you what," he said, lifting his heels slightly, "I'm prepared to take 'em off your hands, right here and now. I'll give ya' fifty dollars cash and cancel your credit card charges on that full tank a' gas you just pumped."

"That's very generous, Sir," Clive said, clearly not meaning it, "but there's no way I'd ever part with my girls."

"I hear you, Son," Mr. Furr countered. "And I'm prepared to double my offer. Make it a hundret, the tank full of gas and I'll throw in all the snacks and soda pop you and yer Buddy can chow down between here and New York."

Clearly this was upsetting Clive. He was anything but amused. "Mr. Furr," I interjected, "we don't wanna sound like we're bein' ungrateful, but the dogs are not fer sale. Pure and simple. Not now ner never. Now, if you'd be so kind as to head us in the right direction, we'd be mighty grateful."

Mr. Furr's tone changed abruptly. "Now, that's too darn bad fer them sweet puppies," he snarled. "I mean, where they gonna run in New York City? They'd have a real good life with Minnie and me here in the country."

"I'm sure," Clive snapped. "But they'll have to take their chances with me." As he jumped behind the wheel, he muttered, "Sweet Jesus, get in and let's clear the fuck out of here."

"I've jotted down yer plates, Boys," Furr announced, menacingly. "Just in case there's any Tomfoolery afoot. The Sheriff's a good friend of mine."

"No doubt, Mr. Furr, but, if I was you, I wouldn't waste my time or the Sheriff's. Only crime we committed was getting lost in Michigan." I was struggling to close the door when Clive put peddle to the metal and sped us away from the station.

"That SOB wouldn't take no for an answer," he grunted.

"Mr. Furr gives new meaning to *creepy local*," I said.

"And what's with that cracker accent of yours?" Clive sputtered. "Nearly had me gagging."

"When he addressed us as 'boys,' I thought he deserved to be responded in kind—imitation being the highest form of flattery."

"Or mockery, depending on who is doing the imitating."

"Whatever. Let's change the subject. After all those detours and wrong directions, I'm starving."

"Truth be told, so am I," Clive nodded.

"Can't be that hard to find our way back to the 80," I assured him. "What do you say we stop for lunch?"

"Here in Badger's Ass? You know something I don't?"

"We're in Coldwater, Michigan. Badger's Ass is much further north," I teased.

Clive pointed to a billboard. "There's something called *China One*."

"How propitious is that?" I asked in my cheeriest voice. "We both love Chinese."

Clive allowed a hint of a smile to appear. "We survived seafood in Iowa, why not Chinese in Michigan?"

"That's the spirit! Hope they have Moo goo gai pan on their menu."

The arrow beneath the sign pointed to a narrow road separating a Midas Muffler shop from a Dunkin' Donuts. In need of serious scraping, the road crossed a vast field that appeared to be freshly furrowed. China One, reminiscent of a rundown Tara, loomed several hundred yards from the highway, fronted by a huge parking lot, empty save for a shiny pick-up truck and a rusting Dodge Dart.

"Looks like it might be closed," Clive observed.

"Pull up by the front door," I said. "I'll run in and check it out."

The cavernous lobby was empty with nary a person in sight. An arched trellis sprouting silk chrysanthemums and plastic ferns framed the Formica-topped reception desk which looked to have been long abandoned from its original purpose. A floor-to-ceiling, mica-flecked fountain adorned the wall behind it, its pump whining for want of water. Cardboard 'To-Go' containers were stacked waist high in its basin.

"Hello. Hello," I called out. "Anybody here?" When no one answered, I looked around for a bell or buzzer and noticed a crayoned sign taped to the desk top: 'Pull dragon for service,' it instructed. In a bow to its Oriental motif, a ceramic dragon's head dangled at the end of a length of clothes line which, after passing through a pulley mounted near the ceiling, disappeared into areas unknown. I gave it a yank and a gong sounded in the distance. "Hold your horses," a female voice called out. "With you in a minute."

"You open for lunch?" I asked the rail-thin teenager shouldering her way through the swinging door.

"Yah, long as you don't order anything too complicated," she replied with a pout.

"Great. If you can wait a second, I have to let my friend know it's okay to park and come on in."

"Not goin' anywhere," she sniffed.

Outside, when I informed Clive, he said, "That's good, but the girls badly need their Stretch and Poop. I'll be in shortly. If they have Egg Foo Young, go ahead and order it for me, with a couple of spring rolls and a side of brown rice."

Returning to the lobby, I asked for the young woman's name and if I might look at a menu. "The cashier called in sick this morning," she explained, "then the busboy called in sick and our regular cook has a funeral in his family. So, I'm here all alone, except for the fry cook. My name's Sharlene, spelt with an S, by the way. Lost my name tag a couple weeks back. Been too busy to get another one."

"Sorry to hear all that, Sharlene with an 'S,' but do you mind if I ask, why is your place so empty? Are we *that* late for lunch?"

"Nah. Mostly we do take-out these days. After the foundry shut down, business has been really slow for everybody in town. Local folks don't eat out near as much as they used to."

"Got it. So where would you like us to sit?"

"We got three dining rooms. You got the whole place to yourself—sit any place you like." With that, Clive appeared and ordered Egg Foo Young. I ordered Moo Goo Gai Pan, and asked for extra snow peas, but Sharlene didn't seem to know what snow peas were and was sure they didn't have any nor had they ever. Clive and I decided to split an order of egg rolls and share his order of brown rice. Then we wandered around, finally settling on a corner table in the huge room at the rear of the building.

"Good God!" I exclaimed. "The size of this place!"

"Looks like Jackie Chan's version of The Shining," Clive observed and pointed to a Fire Marshall sign:

MAXIMUM
OCCUPANCY
NOT TO EXCEED
140 PERSONS

"We'd better eat up and run," I cracked. "Chinese restaurants are notorious fire traps." After a prolonged wait, during which we pondered the possibility that Sharlene had driven to another Chinese restaurant to pick up our meal, she arrived with enormous, spilling-over-the-plate portions and the hand-written check. My Moo goo gai pan was embroidered with a dozen miniature corn-on-the-cobs—I assumed, to make up for the alien snow peas.

Throughout the meal, we shook our heads, amazed at how bizarre the day's events had become. When it came time to pay the check ($12.10 plus a $3. tip) Sharlene was nowhere to be found.

"You need a Sherpa guide to find your way out of this place," Clive cracked as we stumbled our way back to the lobby. Hoping to summon Sharlene, he gave the Dragon's head a pull, but as he did, it broke lose from the rope and fell to the floor. "Perfect ending to a perfect meal," he mused.

"Confucius say: dropping Dragon head on floor bring seven years bad luck to round eye Guy."

"And impotence to politically incorrect gray-hair Guy," Clive hissed. When Sharlene appeared, he handed her the Dragon's head and said he was sorry—he didn't think he'd pulled it *that* hard.

"Don't worry, happens all the time," she consoled him, adding that, "the credit card machine is 'on the fritz' so I hope you guys don't mind paying in cash?"

"You think the MSG might have gotten to it?" Clive wondered.

"Not necessarily. Could be something in the Coldwater water," I offered. Between giggles, we cobbled together two fives and five ones and thanked Sharlene for her service.

"Tomorrow's my day off," she sighed. "This'll help. My boyfriend's taking me to his chiropractor, then I'm gettin' my hair permed and we end up at his step-Dad's BBQ."

"I envy you the chiropractor part," Clive nodded.

"Really?" I said, tongue firmly in cheek. "I've never had a perm. Can't imagine what that must be like."

"I'll give you a hint," Clive sniffed. "First you have to have hair."

Sharlene stared at us intently, wavering between a frown and a smile. "For two older guys, you're pretty funny. If you don't mind my asking, do you always talk to each other like that?"

Clive flashed his wickedest smile, and I knew we were in for a doozey of a response. "Thank you for asking, Sharlene," he purred. "You see, besides being older guys, we're also Gay guys, so it's in our genetic makeup to be funny 24/7."

Sharlene's jaw dropped. "I'm sorry, I didn't mean to…"

"No offense," he assured her. "To be perfectly honest, my friend is much, much older than I am and consequently, much, much gayer. Can't help himself. Comes with age. But I don't hold it against him. Nor do I let him hold *anything* against me. I just try to keep my end up, particularly when we do a long road trip like this one." With that, he kissed me on the forehead, took my hand and pulled me toward the door. "Come along, Sweetie," he lisped. "We have to find you a drug store—you're down to your last two Depends," and trotted me across the parking lot.

"Jesus, and you say I'm outrageous," I gasped, choking from laughter.

"Not a peep until we're in the car," he commanded.

Sharlene stood in the door, hand cupped to her forehead. "Ya'll come back and see us, next time you're passin' through," she shouted. Fully expecting him to speed away in a cloud of dust, Clive surprised me by blowing her a kiss and gently easing the Rover onto the road.

"Brother, when you decide to show your colors, pink and purple never had a campier spokesman," I said.

"Thank you, but I regard my style as creative rather than campy."

"My only question is why waste it on that unsuspecting child? I think you just confused the hell out of her."

"Or gave her something to talk about while she's having her perm."

"Which is how this started. What's with calling attention to my hairpiece?"

"I only did it because it's so damned good. I guarantee she had no idea what I was talking about."

"Much older? Much Gayer? He can't help himself.' I take it I'm no longer allowed to be offended by anything you say?"

"Like you're always telling me, lighten up, C. Bobby. You know you loved it."

"Of course I did, but I still think you owe me big time—making me the butt of your Rainbow Rant—your 'gay whipping boy.' As one matures, one's dignity becomes more fragile, therefore more easily bruised. I'm nothing if I don't have my dignity."

"Tut, tut, touchy! This from the man who gets the giggles at a midnight mass and once likened holy communion to metaphorical cannibalism."

"I deeply regret having confessed those observations to you, and will henceforth deny them."

"Martin Luther would be proud. Anyway, I remembered a few more details about how Tom and I first met. If you'll come down off your wounded high-horse, I'll share them with you."

"Thank you. My high-horse tires easily these days, especially when wounded."

"The next day after Tom slipped us his number, Wayne called him and Tom offered to get us invited to a Hollywood party—scheduled to take place on the following Sunday."

"And did he?"

"Yes. Turned out to be a pool party at Henry Willson's—the famous agent. Never forget that evening. I was more naïve than you can imagine and in complete awe. Apparently, Willson had been pursuing Tom for years, but he resisted all his offers of representation and remained loyal to Dick Clayton, his first agent. Willson was so worried about reporter's hiding in the bushes, his 'Beefcake' clients were on standing orders to arrive with a female on their arms. Willson said that three men always translated as a night out with the boys, but two men read as a date. The women, mostly starlets and studio secretaries, were referred to as 'beards' by anyone in on the game."

"I read about those pool parties in someone's autobiography. Can't remember whose."

"By having Wayne and me arrive on his arm, Tom was stretching Willson's rule, and at the same time defying it. Of course, I knew none of this, at the time. When we arrived, it was mostly men with a few women standing around."

"Seems so totally paranoid, now," I grumbled.

"True, but remember, the studio bosses had invested thousands in promoting guys like Rock Hudson, Tab Hunter and Guy Madison into household names. They were anxious to protect their investment."

"I remember reading that, after sipping a cocktail and chatting with Willson for a few minutes, the 'beards' were chauffeured home by one of his drivers."

"It was certainly true that night. After the last girl left, those of us who had not already done so were invited to change into bathing suits that Willson provided and jump in the pool. So I found myself swimming with Rock Hudson, Tab Hunter, Guy Madison, John Saxon, Race Gentry, Cal Bolder, Clint Connors, and a pair of twins who Willson had renamed Dirk and Dack Rambo. Tom pointed out later that he and I were the only people in the pool with real names."

"Wow—what an HBO movie that would make!"

"Tom referred to that evening as 'The Stirring of the Stew.' I guess it worked because a couple of days later, Wayne got a call from Dick Clayton, Tom's agent—one of the best in Hollywood. Everyone regarded Dick as the classier version of Henry Willson. We made a handshake deal until my Mother could sign the contracts and Dick immediately began to work his butt off for me."

"Clayton's still with us, isn't he?"

"Yes, and still highly regarded. Retired from the agency business just a couple of years ago."

"I'm going to need a pit stop pretty soon," I warned. "The map says Sandusky is just ahead—I assume you know what the town is famous for?"

"No, but let me guess. Sand and dusk?"

"Rollar Coasters. Sandusky calls itself the roller coaster capital of the world. Cedar Point is their amusement park and it's supposed to have the steepest, fastest roller coasters in the world."

"You said you needed a pit stop, not a..."

"It's Friday afternoon—it's bound to be open. I love roller coasters. Come on, what do you say?"

"I say you're out of your fucking mind."

———

"The biggest, the tallest, the fastest!" I cheered. "Everybody's a size queen when it comes to roller coasters. How can you resist?"

"Everybody but me. If you'd like, I'll drop you off at the next exit. You can thumb your way to Cedar Point and ride their coaster's until you've thrown up to your heart's content."

"It's nothing like that, and you know it. Besides, how would I get to New York?"

"Frankly, my dear, I don't give a damn."

"Yes you do. Your tough guy act is not your long suit, Mr. Wilson—despite the rumors that continue to swirl about your early days with Tom."

"Does that mean we're done with the roller-coaster riff?"

"Only 'cause you're such a cowardly party pooper."

"I resemble that remark. What rumors and swirled about by whom? Tom's been gone for over a decade and so many of our friends have followed him. Who's left to do the swirling? Names, please?"

"Trent, Michael, Brian, for instance."

'Why am I not surprised? Sounds like somebody failed 'Getting a life, 101."

"They weren't gossiping. They said even Tom's friends were concerned over how you two could possibly make it work. Trent said he gave it six weeks at the most."

"Obviously La Trent was wrong. I don't know about the others but it strikes me as a pointless topic, after all these years."

"I've always wanted to hear your version of the story—the one you first recounted to Jerry Powell, our accompanist, and you vaguely referenced to me, a couple of times."

"Which story was that?"

"About Tom's insistence on you being circumcised."

"Leave it to you, C. Bob. What more apropos subject to replace not getting to ride a roller-coaster?"

"You told Jerry you were 18 at the time." With that, Maggie and Georgie commenced to whine.

"Saved by the bell," Clive cheered. "Sounds like we could all use a rest stop, right about now."

"That's fine. It's my turn to take the wheel, anyway." As if by telekinesis, a sprawling 'Visitor Center' appeared over the next rise. We pulled in, agreed upon a civilized 15 minutes for everyone to relieve themselves, after which the dogs chased a dray of squirrels up a tree; I scraped my wrist prying a bag of Cheetos from a malfunctioning snack dispenser and Clive assumed a look of stoicism I'd not seen before. Back on the road, with me at the wheel, it seemed provident to say nothing—hoping my uncharacteristic silence would serve to honor his. Eventually it worked.

"For you and you alone, I've decided to tell all, C. Bobby. Though for what real purpose, I haven't the vaguest."

"I'm honored. I'll do my darnedest not to interrupt unless I'm confused."

"I won't hold my breath," he mumbled. "Tom and I had been together three or four months. I'd followed him on a couple of press junkets for "The Cardinal." Usually separate flights. Remember, he was a thirty-seven-year-old star, still under contract to Preminger— and, at 6' 3", stood out in every crowd. I was 5' 6', an eighteen year old singer/ dancer and…"

"Drop-dead gorgeous," I interjected.

"Sweet and totally subjective, C. Bobby. You didn't have to be a studio exec or a press agent to calculate the potential bombshell our relationship presented to anyone promoting Tom's career."

"Brian says he met you the first time in '62 or '63, at a cocktail party in London. He was a student at the University of Glasgow, had met Tom a couple of years before and was impressed with his beauty and intelligence. Brian was told by the English host, "Wait until you meet this young chap he's with. His name is Clive. You'll like Tom even better. He brings out the best in Tom.""

"Brian's got it partially right. Except I wasn't along for that London trip. Tom was still in a relationship with Donald McCleary— he was principal dancer with the Royal Ballet—so my name was not to be mentioned in polite company."

"Sounds too scandalous. Do I need smelling salts for what's coming next?"

"Maybe. Tom hated that I wasn't circumcised. Insisted if we were to continue, I had to undergo the procedure—which, after meeting with several doctors, was scary as hell to contemplate. But, as you said about Tony, 'I loved him so much, I'd do anything for him.'"

"Calls to mind that tacky line about…no, I'd better not say it."

"What tacky line?"

"Never mind. Sorry I brought it up."

"No, Motor Mouth. You can't tease me and then not deliver. *What tacky line?*"

"For you, Darling, I'll shorten it a couple of inches."

"Oh, that one. I used it on Tom for years."

"He didn't think it was tacky?"

"How could he? He knew it was true." Clive flashed his wickedest smile. "Now, do you want to hear the rest of the story or don't you?"

"Motor Mouth shutting down."

"The Doctors explained there were two kinds of circumcisions. One was called the 'dorsal slit' technique, where they pull the foreskin forward and cut it off like snipping off the point of a carrot."

"I'm wincing already."

"Well, you asked for it. The other is the 'sleeve' technique where they draw a line beneath the head, then make a circular cut and remove the skin like pulling off a condom."

"Which did you have, I shudder to ask?"

"They decided I was a candidate for the sleeve technique, which requires more stitches and is more difficult to recover from."

"Ouch! I hope they knocked you out for it?"

"No, I was awake. They applied some numbing cream on it, about a half hour before the surgery. After it became numb, a local anesthesia was injected directly into the head."

"Double Ouch! Doesn't sound like a barrel of laughs."

"I could feel it every step of the way, but there wasn't any real pain during the actual procedure. That didn't come until the day after."

"Thank God, my folks had me circumcised when I was just a week old."

"They closed the incision with sutures, then put a bandage on it, soaked with Vaseline jelly. I remember yelling at the doctor because the jelly was so damned cold."

"Is there much more? I'm feeling a bit woozy."

"Open the window. Shot of fresh air will do you good." I did and felt slightly better. "Dare I continue?" Clive asked, clearly relishing my discomfort.

"Yes, but you can leave off the part about removing the bandages and pulling the stitches."

"That's the most interesting part. They warned that if I had an erection before I was completely healed, it could cause the sutures to break and the incision to open up."

"I can't handle much more."

"Said I would need more surgery if that happened."

"And did it? he asked, dreading the answer."

Clive giggled. "Thank God the nurses were all Miss Ratchet types. Before I left the hospital, the doctor had a few more reassurances to give me. 'Your penis may not have as much feeling as it did before,' he said and—this was my favorite—'It may not look the way you expect it to look.' Well, duh! Short of hoping it might be 5 inches longer, what about its look could possibly disappoint me?"

While I struggled to conjure a non-Neil Simonesque response, Clive waved his hand. "Don't answer that, C. Bob. I know how are with anything rhetorical. Anyway, the recovery was not easy!"

"How long before you could try out the...um...revised equipment?"

"I thought you'd heard enough?"

"It's just that you've recounted some of this story before, but never got to..."

"For you, never!"

"Did too—the night we got snockered on Ramos Fizzes in the kitchen at Sunset Plaza. Whipped up so many of them, we ran out of egg whites. Tom roared into the kitchen, saying we were making so much noise we'd ruined his writing session. I said something stupid like, 'I'm so sorry, Tom. I promise we'll cut it off right away.' To which you and I laughed our asses off."

"I remember. I was about to hit you with the blender 'cause Tom had guessed what we were laughing about."

"Okay, so the answer is...?"

"Answer to what?"

"How soon were you able to try out the foreshortened staff and what was it like?"

Clive shook his head. "Always the dog with the bone."

"Or boner," I retorted, to which we both laughed so hard, I was forced to pull off the highway for another unscheduled pee break.

As we made our way into the bushes, Clive chuckled, "No fair trying to sneak a peek!"

"I recall Ring Lardner, Jr. being quoted in one of those wonderful anthologies about screenwriters—Backstory 3, I think it was called. Lardner was talking about doctoring scripts for Otto Preminger and how respectful Preminger was to writers, especially black-listed writers and what a total son-of-a-bitch he could be to actors. Lardner said Preminger was the most abusive to Tom during the filming of *The Cardinal,* and ironically, he thought it was fair to say that Preminger was responsible for turning a limited actor into a successful novelist."

"Lardner has it mostly right," Clive nodded. "*The Cardinal* debacle with Preminger put Tom in the hospital and left him more than a little damaged. And, like me, he loathed having to wait by the phone for his agent to call and tell him some studio exec had finally made up his mind. He was testing for one movie or TV role after another and striking out. To hold onto his sanity, he wrote his first novel—had high hopes for it. 'This could be my ticket out of Hollywood Hell,' he said, over and over. All well and good, but, despite my salary on the Soap, the bills were mounting. Without telling him, I'd gone to the pawnshop on my day off. While I was away, he received a letter of rejection from some asshole film agent who didn't know the first damned thing about writing, and refused to pass Tom's manuscript onto the Literary Department. The letter was lying on the kitchen counter when I came through the door and found Tom with his head in the oven. Jesus, what an awful moment that was! I ran over, turned off the gas, grabbed him around the neck and literally tackled him to the floor. For a couple of minutes, we both cried our eyes out."

Clive wiped his nose on his sleeve. "God damn, this is hard," he said. "Why did I ever let you talk me into telling it?"

"Obviously, you need to get it off your chest, my friend." I could feel tears coursing my cheeks, as well. "It's the classic unburdening process—the raison d'etre for the Catholic confessional, the only part of Scientology that occasionally works."

"You could have gone all day without mentioning Scientology."

"Sorry. Won't do it again, I promise. But, you know it's true. You also know it's not cool to break off in the middle of the incident."

"Yada, yada, yada—I know." he sighed, took a deep breath and continued. "So I grabbed a dish towel, ran it under the cold water and wiped off his face. I assured him that nothing could diminish my love and admiration for him. Told him he was too intelligent for most of the fools running the studios. There was sure to be a great future ahead—but he had to hang in there. Together we'd get through this terrible period—just be a matter of time before he would achieve great success."

"How right you were."

"Finally I made him to smile when I showed him the $200. I'd gotten for my Rolex. 'Look Tom,' I said. 'We can have supper at Scandia tonight and make a serious dent in the long-distance bill tomorrow."

"That's a lovely story, Clive. Proves once again, behind every great man there's usually…another great man."

"Thanks, C. Rob, but I never think of myself as anything like…"

"Remember that long, hand-written letter from Tom you showed me in Hawaii? The one I suggested you should keep for collateral?"

"What about it?"

"I remember saying to you, it was either a profound literary gem or a 'I want my cake and eat it too' declaration for no longer wanting to have you around, fulltime."

"Hardly what I needed to hear, but you've never been bashful with your opinions."

"What ever happened to it?"

"Probably stuck in my files, somewhere."

"Did you ever reread it?"

"Yes, once. It was during that awful period with Cal Culver. At the height of their entanglement, Tom escaped to Paris to avoid being connected to the blind items that were appearing in the gossip columns. Liz Smith and Rona Barrett had both hinted about their affair. Tom was terrified of losing his publisher, and worse, alienating his readers. For some reason, it struck me as a propitious time to revisit our correspondence. I remember thinking his letter was quite profound—certainly more so than when he first handed it to me. As to its self-serving aspects—you were right—there were several of them—but they were offset by his unorthodox ideas for making a long-term relationship work."

"Ever wonder how it might read as a stand alone document?"

"If you mean like 'How do I love thee? Let me count the ways,' I don't think there's any comparison. Anyway, Tom didn't stay in Paris for long, and when he returned to New York, we sat down and hammered out a new understanding of what sharing our lives could be."

"I remember, you wrote me a long letter about it. I was cautiously pleased for you, but afraid the other shoe could drop at any time."

"Shortly after that, I met Michael Bennett at a cocktail party. As the fates would have it, someone had just dropped out of *A Chorus Line* during the final week of rehearsals at Joe Papp's Public Theatre, Downtown. On a whim, Michael offered me the job so I showed up next day, not having a clue what I was getting into. No time for second thoughts. I stepped into the part with barely 6 days of rehearsals. As you know, we were a sensation at The Public—sold out every night—stars like Ingrid Bergman and Rudolf Nureyev came to see us—Nureyev came twice. Wasn't long before the Shuberts brought us to Broadway and the rest, as they say, is history. My life-long dream to be in a Broadway show by age 30 had come true. And, to put the cherry on the icing—that's where I met Rick."

"How did Tom react to that relationship?"

"Thought it was great—referred to Rick as 'your little Twink.' At last, I was earning my own money again—making a decent salary—performing on Broadway eight times a week. What was there to complain about? Exercising my independence became progressively easier. Tom loved the idea that I was standing on my own two feet, no longer dependent on his largess. At the same time, he worried that I might become so independent, I'd leave him for good." Clive paused for a deep breath and grinned. "You just know, I played that card for all it was worth."

"I couldn't help but notice when Tony and I visited you over the Bicentennial weekend."

"Later—I think it was around '86 or '87—Cal Culver was dying of AIDS. He visited Tom at the San Remo—making his 'farewell tour' so to speak. Cal looked like the wrath of God—I felt so sorry for him. Once the beautiful boy-next-door porn star, but by then he was a virtual skeleton. Tom was upset for a long time after his visit. He never said it out loud, but I think it sparked his decision to give up New York and move back to Los Angeles, fulltime."

"According to my reckoning, we've done slightly over 400 miles today," I said. "Considering all the unexpected detours, that's a pretty good day's work. What do you say we pitch our tent?"

"I'm calling the Motel 6 in Youngstown, as you speak."

Source: www.motel6.com

Motel 6 Youngstown, OH #4553
From a friendly check-in to a clean comfortable room, this Motel 6 will exceed your expectations. 4249 Belmont Avenue, I-80 at exit #229/ Belmont Avenue Youngstown, OH, 44505 Phone: (330) 759-4092

After our gourmet feast of 2 taco Supremes and Diet Pepsis at Taco Bell, Clive stopped at a liquor store to buy a fifth of Smirnoff and a bottle of tonic. I had a sip or two of Chardonnay left in our cooler, but didn't feel like drinking anything alcoholic, and made do with tap water.

"What's with the newfound temperance, C. Bobby? We're almost done with our odyssey. Time to celebrate." He held up the bottle. "Have a vodka. Much better for you—it'll take away the taste of that gawd-awful vinegar you've been drinking."

"Thank you, but no thanks. One of us needs to be stony-sober for the final stretch."

"Is that some kind of judgment call? If so, your holier than thou act is a little hard to swallow."

"Not as hard as it's been to watch you swallow God knows how many vodkas every night. And, yes—you can think of that as a judgment call."

"Pardon me, Carrie Nation. I know what I can handle and when to stop." He tilted his glass defiantly and took a big gulp. "When have you ever seen me drunk—even slightly? Never, that's when."

"Never stereotypically soused, that's true. But after your second vodka, you become sarcastic and bitchy, and no fun to be around."

As was his pattern when annoyed, Clive gestured skyward with his glass. "This from the man who holds a BA in bitchy and a Doctorate in sarcasm."

"To my lasting regret, I don't have a degree in anything, as you well know. If we could set the Noel Coward badinage aside for a few minutes—I'm becoming really concerned about the volume of your booze consumption."

"Oh you, are you? And why, may I ask, have you waited until our last night on the road to mention it?"

"Call it cowardice—fear of causing a dust-up between us."

"Dust up? How quaint! I repeat, why now?"

"Because I'm worried about your driving. As we get closer to New York, you know the traffic is sure to increase exponentially. 18 Wheelers everywhere. Driver's are more aggressive. Road Rage is rampant. I shudder every time you swerve in and out of lanes without signaling. Remember, we had two near-misses—one back in Iowa and one in Nebraska."

"Cheap shot, C. Bob! Arbitrarily calling them 'near-misses' to prove your point."

"Happened in the morning—both times. Your hands were shaking—your eyes were blood-shot. I know that's why you wear sunglasses—even when it's overcast."

"Never had a serious accident in my whole life. Never more than a fender-bender or two and it was always the other driver's fault. Matter of record, if you care to look it up."

"What about a DUI? I remember you said you'd gotten one a couple years before we met."

"A hundred years ago. Driving back after a late-night party in Malibu. Tom's lawyer eventually got the charges lowered to a moving violation and I learned my lesson. It's why I only drive at night when I absolutely have to." With that, he poured another.

"Wish I'd remembered to pack my Hazmat suit. Comrade Wilson is on his third vodka."

"And will probably have a fourth—if only to piss off Sister Nation and withstand her sarcasm. I repeat, I've never had a serious accident."

"Hardly puts the odds in your favor, My Prince."

•

Day Seven

A heavy fog shrouded the area when we checked out of the motel and wolfed down breakfast at Denny's, anxious to be on the road by 8:00, with hope of arriving in Manhattan before sundown. Concerned for his trembling hands, I offered to drive, but Clive insisted he was 'just fine and stop sounding like my Mother.' The fog was so thick it made it nearly impossible to read the signs or see beyond a car or two ahead, which kept us both on edge until mid-morning when it finally lifted.

"Oh, my God, Clive! Look what I just found in the bottom of my shoulder bag." I held up a cassette cartridge. "Completely forgot that I had it."

"Just because the fog has cleared doesn't mean I'm ready for the Ring Cycle," he sneered. "Given a choice, I'd *almost* rather listen to Limbaugh."

"Relax, it's not Wagner. It's one of our favorites. My friend Richard made me a dub, just for the trip."

"I'm guessing—Sondheim's 'Company?'"

"More better. Ruth Draper doing *The Italian Lesson.*"

Clive lit up like he'd been hit by a spotlight. "Nel mezzo del cammin di nostra vita, mi ritrovai per una selva oscura," he intoned in Draper's fluty voice, as I inserted the cassette into the player. "Dantes words, like Shakespeare, seemed to know the things that always would be true," he continued.

But, when I hit play, there was only the sound of rushing wind and static. I hit rewind, reinserted the tape, but got more of the same. "When's the last time this thing was cleaned?" I asked.

"How do I know? Haven't used it since I got my iPod."

"Damn and double damn," I fumed. "If anybody could help us through Why-O, Why-O Ohio, it would be Ruth Draper."

"Not to worry—I know practically every word of it," Clive boasted.

"For me, the way she segues from conversing on the phone to speaking to her secretary and her servants, then back to the phone is absolutely flawless."

Clive nodded and continued, "Jane, we shall be eight for dinner tonight and I want a very simple dinner. Have you some clear soup? Put something amusing in it. I don't really mind what." This immediately set us giggling like schoolboys.

"I know you put in eight little pigeons and you put almost everything in with them," I added. "And Jane, do that wonderful thing you do with the little peas and mushrooms."

"And then get dear little Mr. Miller. Well, he's always free you know, and he likes everybody and he likes everything and always…"

I joined in, "…always gives me a feeling of *hope*!" Like the Mary Martin story, quoting Draper had us immediately howling like asylummates.

When he'd caught his breath, Clive continued. "For dessert? I don't know, Jane. Why not just fruit? Fruit and coffee ought to be enough for anybody."

"And when she's on the phone to a friend who's just back from a trip: "How was Mexico? Did you get to Guatemala? One can't call oneself a real traveler without getting to Guatemala."

"And my absolute favorite," Clive gushed, "when she's talking to the painter about her daughter's portrait. 'Yes, Count Blufski, the portrait has arrived and is hanging in the drawing room in the place you selected near the window, and the light is lovely on it. And we're all *crazy* about the frame. But we were wondering, could you put more pink in her cheeks, and put a blue ribbon in her hair to contrast it? It's the summer and it makes her a bit flushed and the heat makes her hair curl. I'm sure you wouldn't mind making those few little changes, Count Blufski? Then everyone will be happy."

"And we're all crazy about the frame," I repeated. "Has there ever been a more brilliant summation of what an artist-for-hire has to endure?"

"Tom saw Ruth Draper in concert. He said her recordings are wonderful, but nothing compared to seeing her live, onstage. She was a true genius."

"Unfortunately, I never heard of her until after she died."

"I'm so tired of making wine from water, loaves from fishes," Clive anguished. "I've been spinning silk purses from sow's ears for so long, it seems like forever since I've had any real income."

"If you'll recall, an earlier version of this speech lured me into making this trip with you."

"Yeah, but there's more. Tom left me his works to till and harvest, but I'm not the literary farmer he was. You'd think, with mini-series like *Horatio Hornblower* and movies like *Master and Commander*, his *Kingdom Come* quartette would be a natural for adaptation. But I've been unable to drum up a shred of interest from anybody—none of the studios, not HBO or PBS or the BBC—anybody."

"The audience for mini-series, and the appetite for making them is incredibly cyclical," I responded, hoping to sound the sympathetic sage. "The networks haven't been producing period pieces with any consistency, lately. The *Kingdom Come* stories are so epic—would be so expensive to produce, we'll all be long gone before they get made—if ever.

"Now, who's Debbie Downer?"

"Just being realistic," I said, shaking my head. "I'm hearing what my friends in high places have to say about what's selling and what isn't. Just like you, I don't understand why those wonderful sagas weren't snatched up years ago."

By 11:00, having long since crossed into Pennsylvania, my head was throbbing and I insisted we had to stop for a snack. The gluttonous gas tank needed feeding and we were both wanting a break. When a sign pointing to the Milesberg off-ramp appeared, I said, "Looks good as any. Let's do it." We bounced over several sets of train tracks and made our way to the Lehigh Gas station. Clive located a grassy knoll for the girls to do their duty while I filled the tank. After he'd deposited their efforts in a trash can, he grabbed a squeegee and began to clean the windshield.

"I was rereading *Anna Karenina* not long ago," he mused. "What a powerful story!"

"Talk about arbitrary, Clive! Scooping dog poop to wiping the windshield to a book-chat on Anna Karenina? How does your outré mind hitch all that together?"

"Xnay on the outré—it's inapt. It was seeing those locomotives and box cars on the tracks over there."

"I'm not following you."

"Anna Karenina really speaks to me, especially her tragic end. I find it strangely romantic."

"And I find it strange that you find it romantic. Didn't she throw herself under a train?"

"Yes. In the beginning of the story, Anna witnesses a railway worker's accidental death and the image is so vivid, it stays with her for years."

"And that's romantic? More like 'grotesque' if you ask me?"

"In the last chapter, Anna's confusion and vengeful anger overcomes her and, recalling the railway worker's demise, she ends it all by throwing herself in the path of a departing train."

"And you find that romantic?"

"Yes, Dr. Phil. I do. Anna Karenina is Tolstoy's timeless masterpiece—an epic romance." He wiped the last of the dead bugs from the windshield and placed the squeegee back in its rack. "As with all the great classics, you close the cover and put it back on the shelf to savor another time."

"Not so easy for me," I confessed. "I can't help imagining what her body would have looked like, run over by a locomotive."

"Shows how different we are," he shrugged as we climbed into the van. "I lean toward Romance, you run to Grand Guignol."

It was my turn at the wheel and we were well on our way before I spoke. "You spooked me back there, Clive. Mention of suicide always freaks me out. And the idea of jumping under a train…"

"Relax. I'm spit-balling a few ideas to finish one of Tom's short stories—something he started years ago. Anyway, if I were ever to do it, it would be with pills. Everything else is so messy. You'd just have to make sure there are enough of them. Can you imagine what it would be like to wake up after an attempt to end it all?"

"Actually, I know somebody who did. When she recovered, she went back to school, got a degree in child psychology and now she lectures on suicide prevention to High School faculties in the D.C. area. Having been there and back, they say she's a very powerful speaker."

"Perhaps I'm losing my touch, or maybe I never really had it," Clive mumbled.

"How's that?"

"When it comes to finding and holding onto romance."

"Polar opposite of me. My big realization—apotheosis, really—happened after I turned 50. I realized that I was the best lover I was ever going to have, certainly this time around."

"That's fraught with denial, C. Bobby. Don't tell me there isn't a time when you'd rather be snuggling beside something other than a down pillow."

"Actually, my favorite snuggle is my Hawaiian quilt. Yes, there are times, but nothing worth surrendering my solitude or selfish disposition for. Being one's own lover makes for one less person to buy birthday and Christmas gifts for and one more gift for oneself. I liken the joys of living alone to the joys of travelling alone: you don't have to check with anyone when you're done gawking at cathedrals and ready to crash a cocktail hour."

"Are those original aphorisms or are you quoting someone?"

"Probably a bit of both. 'There's nothing new under the sun, only a new way to say it."

"Tom always thought that expression was just a high-minded excuse for literary laziness."

"Was that his original aphorism or was he quoting someone?"

"Touché." Clive looked away for a brief moment. "God how I miss him."

"I can only imagine. All this relates to losing your touch, how?"

"It was that sign pointing to Altoona a couple miles back."

"If this is a test of my attention span, I think I just failed it."

"Oh, shut up! Not everything has to relate to you. About a year ago, I met this guy at the gym—we'd just finished a Spinning class. He dropped one of his gloves—I retrieved it, chased him to the locker room and handed it to him."

"How 'Mr. D'Arcy' of you."

"Not so far fetched. After we got to know each other, Mario admitted, corny as it was, he'd dropped the glove on purpose. Said it was the only thing he could think of, on the spur of the moment, to try and get my attention."

"A case of 'horny goes corny.' But only mildly amusing, I'm afraid."

"Mario's Italian, late forties, stocky, comfortable in his butchness—just my cup of tea."

"Nice plusses. And the minuses?"

"Lives in Altoona, married, with grown kids—has a business that brings him to LA and New York several times a year."

"Geographically challenged *and* a late-bloomer. Rarely do such factors bode well."

"This from the man who, for five years, stayed in a relationship with a raging sociopath from Bogalusa, Louisiana."

"Guilty as charged. However, since Ronnie claims he came out at 16, I'd call him an *early-bloomer*. Gave him a jump-start on perfecting ways to wreak havoc on anyone who tried to befriend him."

"Astute. Now, can I get back to my story?"

"Be my guest. Anything that originates in Altoona is sure to be spellbinding."

"You hitting the 'C' pills again?"

"No, I gave them away as a tip to Agnes and Brittany, back at Council Bluffs."

"And you accuse me of over tipping! Now, can I please finish? As I was saying, Mario always kept his cool, wary of any commitment other than 'wanna meet for a bite at Hamburger Heaven, after class?' Then we'd go back to his room at the Beverly Crest, where he always stayed. Had to be after dark—said he couldn't risk having anyone see us together."

"And you put up with that kind of nonsense in this day and age?"

"Tut, tut, C. Bobby. People in tin houses shouldn't throw can openers. It was after our second tryst—I know how you love that word—Mario said I'd inspired him to think about divorcing his wife. He'd leave her financially secure, of course, but then his love for his three kids got in the way. One of them had just made him a grandfather. Because of that, he said he couldn't bring himself to go through with it."

"How many times have we seen this movie?"

"Many, but it's easy to forget the dénouement when you're playing one of the leads. And it's not like I'd *asked* him to divorce her. At this point in my life, I don't need another picket fence or add to my Spode collection and I told him so. For a while it looked like we might find a way to make it work, though he never gave me his home phone number—only his cell, which he changed every month or so."

"You sure this guy isn't Mafia?"

"Crossed my mind, but how do you ask that question? After our fourth or fifth tryst, Mario talked about buying a condo in the Marina for us, but he said his oldest son was his CPA, so getting the finances and paperwork past him might be dicey. When I suggested he could put the condo in my name, he went ballistic. Said it was obvious I was only after him for his money—maybe even looking for a way to blackmail him."

"If he isn't Mafia, he's doing a damned good imitation."

"I was wrecked. Nothing I could say would convince him otherwise. He never actually told me we were finished, but he stopped taking my calls and changed his number altogether. That was 4 months ago, and I'm still trying to get over him."

"As Estelle Winwood used to say, 'We're well out of that, Tallulah."

"Not quite. I have his secret email address on my computer. After we get to New York and I'm settled in, I'm going to give him one more try."

"Proving we're all gluttons for punishment."

"Thanks for the reminder," Clive sniffed.

"I don't claim to be an exception. Look what I suffered through for 5 years."

"There must be a more appropriate word than 'glutton' to describe it?"

"There is—sort of. When I was researching my novel about Ludwig, I became intrigued with several German words—not so much for their sound, which can be jarringly unpleasant, but for their meaning. Fortunately, someone had put me in communication with a graduate student from the University of Berlin. She was very helpful with pronunciation, translation and defining words with multiple meanings."

"Besides sneaking in a boast about having a student friend in Berlin, this is pertinent to…?"

"To a word I've never heard you use."

"My German is limited to Danke schön and Auf Wiedersehen, with dubious pronunciations of each, so what would that word be, he asks, feigning real interest?"

"*Schadenfreude.* Dictionary definition: the pleasure derived from another's misfortune."

"I agree, it's a wonderful word, but I never use it because I try not to practice it—take pleasure in someone else's pain, I mean. I'd be offended if you think I did."

"Come, come, Clara. One of your favorite expressions, along with 'a lot can happen between now and then' is 'You never get it all.' If that's not a variation of Schadenfreude, I don't know what is?"

"Really! Guess I can't blame that on Gore Vidal, can I?"

"You realize, you've told me two different versions of how you and Tom first met?"

"Probably. I've told the story so many times over the years—there was an expurgated version we worked out, in case the press got too snoopy and there's the PG version I told my family. The truth is so boring, it's not even in the middle. And it was all so long ago, I've forgotten chunks of it."

"Forgotten or did so deliberately?"

"Probably both, but what does it matter?" With that, Clive pretended to stifle a yawn. "Tom appeared in a dream last night and reminded me that he and I first met through Edward and Arthur."

"I don't recall seeing those names in my souvenir program."

"You met Arthur several times. Lived in Tom's guest house for years and served as his de facto editor, right up until his final days."

"Yes. Now I remember...*that* Arthur. Sweet man, but who was Edward?"

"Edward and Arthur were a devoted couple for forty—fifty—God knows how many years. Edward was well off—I think he inherited his family's fortune. They both loved opera, ballet—the theatre. Big patrons of the LA County Museum. They were known for giving lavish dinner parties at their Beverly Hills home."

"And this People Magazine portrait is rambling on to where? Edit, for Christ's sake!"

"I never should have given you permission to quote my 'edit' injunction."

"You never did, but Lordy, it's fun hurling it back at you."

"I'm attempting to give you the unexpurgated version, but if you're too busy...?"

"Too busy with what? You know *unexpurgated* makes me drool. Continuer, s'il vous plait."

"I was 16 when the *Flower Drum Song* tour finished its run in Detroit and moved to the Biltmore in Downtown Los Angeles. Our opening night was a big deal—attracted a star-studded audience, including three Scandinavian princesses, though nobody seemed to know why all three of them happened to be in LA at the same time. Anyway, Arthur and Edward were seated front row center—applauded like crazy—laughed at all the right places and afterwards, came backstage and introduced themselves to the stars. When they asked to meet me, I was surprised and flattered. Remember, the part of Wang San only had one song and dance?"

"I didn't, but if I'd seen you in it, I certainly would have."

"Thank you. I'll take that as an olive branch, but it's too little, too late to expect any kind of sexual favors."

"Provocative—insinuating, but a needless digression. Doesn't serve your story."

"I'll be the judge of that. Anyway, Arthur and Edward couldn't have been nicer or more complimentary. They wanted to know my day off so they could invite me to dinner. Said they had a friend they wanted me to meet—someone very important."

"Enter Thomas Tryon?"

"Exactly. We had Sundays off, back then—not like these days when they have you doing a matinee *and* evening performance on Sunday."

"Clive, you're becoming as bad as me—throwing in all sorts of archival tidbits to tart up the story. Cut to the chase, before I doze off."

"Alright! So Arthur and Edward sent their car and driver to pick up Wayne and me at our hotel—I think it was the Mayfair in Downtown LA—only the stars could afford the Biltmore..."

"You're doing it again. Jump cut to where you're walking through Arthur and Edward's front door."

"You sound like Otto Preminger—always having to be in charge of everything."

"Otto Preminger! How insulting is that?"

"What I'm trying to tell you is we didn't go directly to Arthur and Edward's house. They'd arranged for the driver—after he'd picked us up—to swing by Tom's place in West Hollywood and pick him up. So, there I was, squeezed between Wayne and Tom in the back seat of Edward and Arthur's Bentley."

"Ah, the plot thins..."

"Remember how tall Tom was? Right off the bat, he put his hand on my knee and used my thigh as an armrest."

"What was Wayne's reaction to all that?"

"I think he was so dazzled by Tom's presence, he didn't notice what soon became full-on groping." Clive smiled wickedly. "By both of us. You could call it 'Lust at first sight!'"

"You could, but 'Lust in a Limo' would make for a better marquee."

"Good one, though I'm not sure Tom would have approved."

"Lust—Limo, alliterative, easy to spell on a marquee. What's not to like?"

"At supper, Arthur seated me between him and Edward. 'Think of us as your duennas,' he whispered. 'At least until after dessert,' Edward giggled and gestured to Tom, seated across from me. 'Then you're on you own.' Arthur mouthed."

"Sounds like our little Trinidadian tap-dancer had stepped in high cotton."

"And then some. I'd never seen anything like it: Waterford crystal, sterling silverware, Limoges china, Regency candle sticks and Cymbidium orchids everywhere. Imagine all that *and* Thomas Tryon—The Cardinal—massaging my ankle under the table, with his foot."

"Where was Wayne at this point?"

"Seated next to Tom, but he had his eye on Arthur and Edward's Pilipino houseboy."

"So, did you and Tom make a date for later?"

"Later! Are you kidding? There was no 'later.' Tom promised Wayne he'd get me back to the Mayfair before sunup, called a taxi and whisked me away to his apartment. We barely made it through the door when he literally ripped the pants off me."

"Nice! Say all you want about jumping under trains, Clive, but having your pants ripped off by a handsome movie star—that's what I call romantic!"

"I put a lot of effort into Tom's memorial," Clive mused, "and I was very proud of the way it came off."

"My invitation must have blown off the porch."

"As I recall, you were on location at the time."

"I'll take your word for it. Probably shooting an MOW in Houston or New Orleans. Doesn't matter—so, tell me all about it."

"You would have loved it. I was originally going to hold it at the Bel Air Hotel—down the street from the Stone Canyon house—where you first met Tom. He always loved the Bel Air, but the gardens were already booked with weddings and the cost was way beyond my budget. Then it dawned on me that the perfect spot would be the patio behind the Sunset Plaza house. I hired a harpist to play his favorite music. The weather was perfection. A handful of Tom's closest friends spoke. At the end, we released helium balloons with his initials on them. TT in dark blue letters on pale blue balloons. It was gorgeous."

"Wish I'd been there. I remember loaning you a chunk of money, right after he died. You said it was needed to carry things through until the money from his estate was released. I'm curious, did you use it for the memorial?"

"Oh, God, I don't remember. Tom instructed his lawyers and accountants to set up a bridge-fund to cover any expenses that might crop up immediately after his death. But despite his plans, there was a delay in releasing the money, even from that fund. That's when I called you."

"Fortunately, I was in a position not to need it back right away."

"But I did repay you?"

"Absolutely. I only brought it up because you'd always said Tom had made provisions for you—generous provisions, and yet, there you were, already in a bind, and I was concerned. Worried that maybe something had changed. 'Course I wouldn't think of asking you for specifics at such a difficult time."

"Thank you. It *was* a difficult time—way more than you can imagine. So many details to handle. Even the simplest thing like paying the Gardener seemed to take on an urgency."

"Cute little Mako was afraid you might skip town?"

"Apparently so. Although we were no longer lovers, Rick was very helpful. Don't know how I could have gotten through it without him."

At 12:30 we stopped for lunch at the Country Kitchen in Danville, PA. Knowing it was probably our last meal on the road, we each ordered hearty platters. Clive splurged on a spinach and artichoke omelet while I gorged on a ham and four-Wisconsin cheese omelet. We shared a side of sliced tomatoes and an order of thick French toast. "We'll worry about dieting tomorrow," I said, as I slathered on the butter and syrup.

"Ever feel like you've done all they're going to allow to do in this life?" Clive asked, after he'd signaled for the check.

"Two, possibly three things strike me as flawed in that statement: One—who is *they*? And two, that would imply handing over your power to an unknown."

"And the third, Mr. Suddenly Sanguine?"

"In my experience, the root-cause of 'them allowing or not allowing you to do' anything is rooted in a fear of rejection. Name me one movie, one play, one opera, one painting, one poem, one song, one book, one architectural design—one *language*, for Christ's sake—*that pleases everyone*?" I allowed a lengthy pause for his absorption. "You can't, because there is no such critter. Chances are, every great creative endeavor throughout history was adjudged by some asshole or committee of assholes as being unsuitable, unacceptable or unworthy of their patronage. So, fuck 'em and keep on truckin', that's my motto. And never stop with the 3 Ps—polishing, perfecting and persisting. But, you already know all that, Clive."

"You missed your calling, C. Bobby. Should have been a motivational speaker. You'd be a rich man."

"To which I say, Mr. Speaker, motivate thyself."

As we stood at adjoining urinals, I asked, "How did you manage to land an apartment in the West Village? In a Brownstone on Horatio Street? How great is that?"

"I got lucky. Larry Kert was an old friend. He and his partner, Ron Pullen, have been living in the building for years. After Larry died, Ron stayed on. They have a neat apartment on the third floor. When I realized the only option left for me was to return to New York, I called Ron. He knew a vacancy was about to come up and vouched for me with the owners so I didn't have to weather an intensive credit check."

"So what's the place like? Have you seen pictures?"

"No, but I'm going on Ron's recommendation. First time I've ever rented a place, sight unseen."

"Brave. So, it'll be a surprise for both of us. `What's a studio apartment cost these days—he shudders to ask?"

"$1850. a month, utilities included. I had to put up first and last plus $1,000. as damage deposit—a cool $4700. just to get through the door. But it's a great location—just a couple blocks from the 8th Avenue subway. With any luck, I can be in my office in 15 minutes—even during rush hour."

"You said your company was located in Lower Manhattan?"

"Yeah, in the Wall Street area. About five blocks from the World Trade Center."

"So you were there for 9/11?"

"No, that was the year before I went to work for them."

"Thank God."

"I had just moved into the co-op at Beekman Place—had a mid-morning dentist appointment so I happened to be in the apartment trying to tidy up. June, my roomie, was the sloppiest woman on earth. She would rush out for an audition, always late and always immaculately turned out, leaving behind a trail of dirty clothes and cosmetics scattered all over the place. It was an efficiency studio and her congenital sloppiness, which I didn't realize until we'd gone halfzies on buying the unit, used to drive me crazy."

"An actress for a roommate! What were you thinking?"

"Blood under the bridge. She's supposed to be buying me out, but she's perpetually late with the payments. Drives me nuts. Anyway, our unit was on the 16th floor with a little balcony and I'll never forget the sight of the fighter jets roaring up and down the East River, practically at eye level—the sound rattling the windows and shattering everyone's nerves. Helicopters were swarming like bees. It was a scary morning."

"How close are your offices to Building #7?"

"Don't know. Which one is Building #7?"

"Was! Bldg #7 was the one that came down around 5:20 on the afternoon of 9/11. I think it was also called the Salomon Brothers Building."

"Never heard of it."

"You're not alone. That's why I asked. There's video tape of a BBC newscaster declaring that Building #7 has collapsed—yet it's still standing behind her. The chyron running across the bottom of the screen says it was 4:35 when she made her announcement. But it was a good half-hour before the 47 story, city block square building collapsed in its own footprint—in 6 ½ seconds! Any of this ringing a bell?"

"Can't say it does." Clive shook his head and stared out the side window. "I gather you're a conspiracy theorist," he mumbled. "And why doesn't that surprise me?"

"Nobody delivers a dismissive tone better than you, Clive," I fumed. "Don't be so quick to call me a conspiracy theorist. What the hell is the official *9/11 Commission Report* if it isn't a conspiracy theory? In it we're asked to believe that 19 young middle-Eastern men, who failed at piloting a Cessna, were able to flummox the entire national defense and security systems and steer huge jets into the middle of two 100 story towers and the Pentagon."

"Have any idea what a nut case you're beginning to sound like?"

"Any idea what a sheeple that makes you sound like for swallowing the official story? Never in all modern history has a steel building collapsed from fire. There have been towering infernos that burned for 48 hours, but their steel frames remained standing."

"I assume you have research to backup your theories?"

"Bet your ass I have. And I'm certainly not the first person who questioned the sheer absurdity of the President of the United States taking time away from being leader of the free world to read *My Pet Goat* to kindergarteners in Sarasota."

"I get your point, but for such a conspiracy to happen, how many people would have to be in on it and then keep their mouth's shut for the rest of their lives?"

"Not so many," I snapped. "It's the military's job to follow orders, so it's not so hard to imagine. Forty years later, we're still waiting for the real story on the JFK assassination. 'Magic bullet' indeed! Thank you, Arlen Spector."

"How does stewing over the nightmare of 9/11 in any way make your life better? Or mine? Seems like we already have enough crap on our plates without piling on any more."

"I know it's difficult to wrap your brain around the idea that factions of our own government could conspire to do such a thing. Which is precisely how they got away with it. It's called 'Black Flag.' Create massive shock and awe followed by the biggest lie and cover-up ever—then make it unpatriotic, even treasonous to question any aspect of the tragedy. Whoever the conspirators were ripped pages straight from Goebbels' and Hitler's playbook."

"Got it. Now, can we please change the subject? Even Maggie and Georgie are becoming annoyed with you."

"My fondest wish is that I live long enough to see the whole plot revealed and the culprits brought to justice."

"Don't hold your breath."

It was exactly 4:30 when we inched our way down the ramp leading to the Lincoln Tunnel. The curved approach offers a panoramic view of the Manhattan skyline which never fails to make me gasp and catch my breath. Despite being heavily overcast, that day was no exception. Even Maggie and Georgie seemed to recognize where we were and erupted in joyful barking and yowling. Our enervating seven day odyssey was nearly over.

Soon as we entered the tunnel, I couldn't help myself and crooned in full voice, 'Clive's little town blues—are melting away. He's gonna make a brand new start of it in old New York. If he can make it there, he can make it anywhere. Come on, come through, New York, New York.'

Clive shook his head. "Even a rhinestone blazer couldn't help that rendition, but I thank you and Liza for the sentiment."

In contrast to my excitement, I couldn't help noticing the crude work lights dangling from wires strung along the ceiling of the tunnel and how grungy the tiles looked. "The Lincoln Tunnel janitors might want to ask the guys at the Eisenhower Tunnel what their cleaning secrets are."

"Having a gazillion more cars and trucks passing through it every day, might have something to do with it," Clive sneered. "I mean, Duh."

Fifteen minutes later, we arrived at Horatio Street and were lucky to find a parking space directly across from his townhouse. I was dispatched to fetch change for the meter and some bottled water while Clive met with the owners in their basement apartment. When I returned, he was waiting on the stoop with a professorial-looking senior.

"Bill, this is my friend C. Robert." As we shook hands, I was taken by Bill's ice blue eyes and kindly smile. "Bill and his partner Tom, co-own the building," Clive explained. "He's ready to show us the apartment, now." We entered the tiny foyer and climbed a half-flight of stairs to the door marked 2R. Bill handed a set of keys to Clive, explaining that both the dead bolt and the lock in the doorknob worked with the same key.

"Go ahead—you try opening it," Bill urged. "I just had this set made for you, so let's make sure everything's working right. The previous tenant had trouble with the deadbolt. Claimed it was always sticking—particularly when he was in a hurry."

The door opened easily with Clive's first try and we stepped into a small but tidy room that boasted hardwood floors, a non-working fireplace with marble mantel, and best of all, two tall windows facing west, allowing a partial view of the Hudson River. Bill showed us the butler kitchen concealed behind bi-fold shutters, one fairly large clothes closet and the tiny bathroom with a stall shower. "You have to watch out for the hot water," he warned. "It can get very, very hot, so be careful." Clive was pleased to see the two plastic-wrapped mattresses leaning against the wall. "They were delivered this morning," Bill explained, "but there was no sign of a bed frame."

"It's a trundle bed," Clive explained, "and they warned me it would be arriving separately." Bill handed me a pair of rubber wedges and explained exactly how the front door was to be propped open so as not to scratch the paint or spring a hinge. He added that Tom, his partner, was at his yoga class but would be back in about an hour and bring the lease up for Clive to sign, if that was convenient. With that, he bid us good luck getting everything hauled inside before it got too dark and disappeared down the stairs.

After walking the dogs around the stately, tree-lined block, we commenced to unload the Rover and finished around 8:00. Between schleppings and signing the lease, we measured the room, found it to be 16' X 14 ½' with 11' ceilings. Clive immediately made plans to mirror the wall surrounding the fireplace, measured for two wooden

'Plantation-style' blinds and mentioned replacing the ancient Philco refrigerator with a compact. I took all this as a clear sign of enthusiasm for making the small space livable and stylish, as only Clive could, with his keen eye and sure touch.

"It's 5:00 o'clock in Malibu. Take a minute and call your Mother," I suggested.

"Yes, Warden," he shrugged and grinned when he got her answering machine. He left a detailed message, explaining that we'd arrived safely—the dogs were happy—Greenwich Village was in full bloom and gorgeous—the apartment was going to work out just fine, he loved her lots and he'd try to call again, later.

For supper, we shared a smoked turkey wrap, a fruit salad and a bag of corn chips from the corner deli. Afterward, we located the sheets and towels, stripped the plastic from the mattresses, placed them side by side on the floor, and shortly before midnight, switched off the lone tensor lamp.

"Big day tomorrow," Clive said. "Driving to Jennifer's—retrieve some of my treasures. With any luck, I'll have this place looking like something by tomorrow night."

"I have not doubt," I mumbled and was asleep moments later.

Day Eight

As promised, the ride up to Katonah was relatively short. Before we merged from the West Side Highway onto the Saw Mill Parkway, the light Sunday traffic allowed for exhilarating glimpses of the Hudson River through the blossoming trees.

First glance at Jennifer Haviland's family home, a 2 ½ story, Victorian-styled farmhouse, perched on a slight incline and surrounded by Maple trees, gave the feeling it would have fitted comfortably anywhere in the Midwest. Seeing the Rover pull into her narrow driveway, Jennifer emerged from the screened-in side porch and ran to greet us.

"Clive, darling. You look wonderful," she exclaimed. "How do you manage it after such a long trip?"

"Smoke, mirrors, clean living," he smiled. How are you doing, Jennifer?"

"I'm fine. Working too hard but what's new?" She turned to me. "You must be the C. Robert I've heard so much about?"

"None other. And you're obviously the Jennifer. It's a pleasure."

"Clive, I'm afraid, you'll have to keep the dogs outside, for the time being," she cautioned. "Can't let them near my cats. I have three of them now and the one called Sheba is very sick—don't know if she'll make it through the week. The sight of a dog might kill her."

"No problem. I'll tie them under the arbor, away from the house and out of the sun."

"Perfect!" Jennifer exclaimed. "Now, where do you want to start?"

"Like I said on the phone, Horatio Street is totally unfurnished so I'll need to confiscate quite a few things," he warned her.

As we strolled around the house, identifying items to be carted away, I was struck by the contrast of Jennifer's homespun art and folksy furniture with Clive's Post-Modern prints, Lucite end tables, and chrome apothecary lamps. At the back of the house, Jennifer had transformed the sun room into a veritable showcase of Clive's treasures—as if a Manhattan Penthouse had been transported, virtually intact, to Katonah, Kansas. Also, it was obvious that Jennifer was more than a little infatuated with him. When that realization hit me, I remember thinking, 'Join the queue, Jennifer. Join the queue.'

Once again, we loaded the Rover to its roof—this time with chairs, lamps, a large Chinese urn filled with silk poppies, a drop-leaf table that would serve as Clive's desk and dining table, a few kitchen utensils and several large paintings, the most impressive being the ornately framed Morris Broderson watercolor titled 'For Joan' and Clive's own* 'Heartland #1.'

By 1:30, we'd finished and, as usual, I was feeling ravenous. Jennifer suggested Peppino's—'the only decent place in town open on Sunday.' Located in the heart of Downtown, she extolled its charms and that her family had been going there for years. I rode with her, Clive and the dogs followed us in the Rover. The understanding was, if he elected to have a cocktail or two, I would become the designated driver—stick with iced tea and drive us back to the city.

Best laid plans gone awry: 2:00 pm marked the Brunch-to-Evening shift-change for Peppino's wait and kitchen staff, so it took us forever to get menus and place our orders. By the third time Clive recited his 'Bloody Bull—fresh bullion, Worchester and Tabasco on-the-side' litany, I was ready to devour the leftovers from the next table. The tardy service put Jennifer on the defensive. She kept repeating how embarrassed she was, despite our assurances that we knew it wasn't her fault.

After settling the bill—divided three ways—we bid farewell. Clive alerted Jennifer that he'd be returning the next weekend for a few more items. When we walked around the corner to the Rover, I was expecting him to hand me the keys, but, instead, he climbed in the driver's seat and started the motor. Before I could protest, he said, "Not to worry. I'll be fine. I ate a lot of bread."

"That's reassuring. I thought I was supposed to drive?"

"Relax, I know the fastest way to get us there—I've made this trip I don't know how many times."

Traffic on the return ride was considerably more intense—100s of folks returning home from their weekend in the country—plus convoys of 18 wheelers making their way to Monday morning deliveries. I was about to ask Clive how long he'd known Jennifer and how close was their relationship when he pulled his iPod from his pocket and inserted its ear buds. Whatever he was listening to seemed to affect his accelerator foot and we were soon exceeding the speed limit by 10 or 15 miles.

"For God's sake, slow down, Clive," I shouted. "You're making me nervous."

"Just going with the flow—trying not to get run over." Suddenly, our vehicle veered far to the right, jumped the curb and scraped the metal guard rail so badly, sparks were flying.

"Goddamn it, Clive! Watch where you're going! You trying to get us killed?"

"That Hummer passed too close—he forced me over."

"Bullshit! It's those goddamned Bloody Bulls. And you know it! You're totally buzzed and not focusing on the road. Maybe you have some kind of death wish, but I certainly don't."

"Look, I'm sorry. I'll slow down, I promise. I'll be more careful."

"And put that fucking iPod away. I'm sure it's as against the law here as it is in California."

Seemingly chastened, Clive slowed to just under the speed limit. We finished the last half hour in strained silence, arriving at Horatio Street at 4:30, as lightening flashed and heavy rainfall began to deluge the area. I suggested we rest a bit and let the storm pass before attempting to unload the Rover. Clive quickly agreed.

With the placement of the desk/table between the windows, arranging the chairs and hanging the two largest paintings, Clive was encouraged enough to place a delivery order for a gourmet pizza and Caesar's salad, which we savored while seated at the freshly polished table. Since I was scheduled to take the Rover to New Jersey in the morning, I made no comment about his vodka consumption.

*'Heartland #1' by Clive Wilson is reproduced on the cover.

Day Nine

I was stepping from the shower when Tom, co-owner of the townhouse, banged on the door to inform Clive that the Rover was about to be towed. I threw on my clothes—fortunately I'd repacked my bag the night before—ran to the street, tossed it onto the passenger seat and took off at 8:20. Alas, we'd already received a $65. parking ticket and an $85. citation for an expired inspection stamp. Not anticipating the brutal Monday morning traffic, I spent nearly an hour sandwiching the Rover into the Lincoln Tunnel, panicked that the gas was about to give out any minute. Immediately after merging onto the New Jersey Turnpike, I pulled into the service area, fueled up, consumed a greasy breakfast and called Mother to ask if she had any plans for lunch. She was thrilled to hear that I would be pulling into her driveway in a couple of hours.

When Mother showed me the flyer from the Chinese restaurant that had opened where the landmark Carleton House Hotel once stood, I invited her and Harry, her gentleman friend, to experience its 30 item lunch-buffet. This proved not so simple for two 88 year olds: too many choices of unfamiliar fare while struggling to balance a tray and plates and clutch walkers and canes. Sizing up the problem, I convinced them to sit at the table while I brought an assortment of items to them. By the end of the meal, having pretended we were having a swell time, we agreed that future Chinese banquets would be ordered by phone, for home delivery.

At five minutes to 6:00, I remembered that I had an over-the-phone Pacemaker test with Kaiser, scheduled for 3:00 pm, Pacific Time. I ran to the Rover, retrieved the test box and dialed the clinic, with seconds to spare. The kindly nurses and technicians declared that, despite a minor flutter or two, my heart and its battery was good for another couple of months.

On Tuesday I played telephone tag with my lawyer in Los Angeles; made preliminary plans for shipping art and furniture to New Orleans after settlement with the El Mirador management was finalized; called my Los Angeles phone and retrieved an inquiry regarding my availability to design a TV movie. On learning the filming location was yet to be determined, I convinced the producer to FedEx the script to New Orleans so that I might advise on the decision. I treated two school chums for a late lunch at the Tuckerton Seaport Museum and made awkward jokes about arriving at an age where we looked more like our parents every day. Throughout the afternoon and evening, I placed calls to Clive's cell phone which went unanswered.

That evening, Mother cooked her signature supper of pork chops, sauerkraut, mashed potatoes, green beans and homemade corn bread. After dinner, I offered to do the dishes while she and Harry played Gin Rummy. Harry wisely let Mother win most every hand. After he bid us goodnight, she and I talked at length about how I should be putting something aside for my retirement and how she wanted to die in the house that she and Daddy built. "You and your sister have to promise you'll never put me in one of those old folk's homes," she thundered. Having been drafted onto that winless battlefield many times before, I nodded, crossed my fingers behind my back and said I'd do my best to honor her wish. We retired at 11:30, quite late for Mother. I entered a few notes in my Daytimer and fell asleep shortly after midnight.

Around 4:00 am, I awoke from a horrifying nightmare in which Clive was attempting to take his life by snorting cocaine from a caper-jar and ingesting a fistful of sleeping pills. My wailing roused Mother, who burst into the bedroom, thinking someone had broken into the house. I apologized—said it was only a stupid dream—nothing to concern herself with, but after she returned to her room, I couldn't stop shaking or get back to sleep.

On Wednesday, I called Clive throughout the morning, to no response and, at noon, left for New York, emerging from the tunnel at 2:30. I was just a few blocks away from Horatio Street when he finally answered—explained that he was about to take the dogs for a walk, that the front door key would be under the topiary to the right of the door and he'd left the apartment door unlocked. As to why he hadn't answered before: "My battery went dead—I left the charger in the glove-compartment, so bring it in, if you wouldn't mind. Ron Pullen has the same phone and let me borrow his charger."

Luckily, I found a parking space around the corner on Jane Street, and briefly wondered why Clive hadn't waited a few more minutes until I'd walked through the door. When I tossed my duffle bag into a corner, I was startled by how much smaller the room seemed, compared to first viewing. Clive had taken down the ornate Broderson piece and replaced it with a black and white graphic of a giant egg. I found an Avian in the fridge, sat at the table trying to sip slowly and noticed a small pile of papers stacked next to the computer. Beneath receipts and bills and the lease agreement, I found what, at first glance, looked to be an attempt at a 'farewell' note with no indication as to when it had been written. Scripted in block letters, it began, 'Please be happy for me, and make no effort to…' Here it broke off and several words were crossed out. Eventually, I deciphered; 'Tired of making this journey alone, tired of…and sure there's a better…' 'Good Christ!' I gasped. 'How prescient was my nightmare?' Hearing Clive and the dogs on the stairs, I shoved the paper back in the stack.

We embraced, mumbled our greetings as Maggie and Georgie growled theirs while I argued with myself about if and when to bring up the discovery. Clive chattered on about what a nice long walk they'd enjoyed—how much he loved being back in New York in the spring with all the flowers blooming, shook ice cubes from a tray and poured himself a generous vodka. "So how did it go with your Mother?" he asked through his first long sip.

"Fine. Sends her love to you and…" On the brink of tears, I broke off, seized the note from the pile and held it up. "Clive, what's the meaning of this? I deserve an explanation!"

After a stagey pause, he shot back, sounding anything but caught off-guard, "You are such a Drama Queen! And what are you doing, snooping around my papers, anyway?"

"You can hardly accuse me of snooping, Clive. You left everything right here on the table."

"I was about to put them away when you called," he mumbled, sounding a trace defensive.

"Well, what is this, then? The way you've been acting lately, you're scaring the hell out of me."

"I'm sorry for that, but I'm sure I mentioned about discovering several unfinished manuscripts buried at the bottom of Tom's 'discard' trunk. Once Tom put word to paper, he rarely threw anything away. His agent thought there might be enough stuff to assemble a collection of short-stories and asked me to sort through them, which I've been doing for months." He winked at me and flashed his 'it's no big deal' smile. "The agent is particularly fond of the story about a cable talk show hostess who fakes her own kidnapping and, after she's exposed, threatens suicide." He reached to take the paper from my hand. "I have no idea how long ago I made these notes. Came across them after you left on Monday."

"Wow!" I blurted out. "Either you have an amazing ability to compartmentalize—given all that's on your plate, or your pants are about to burst into flames." Instantly regretting the accusation, I sputtered, "Oh, how I want to believe the former."

If glares could lacerate, I would have been gushing blood. "Believe what you want," he fired back as he tore the page into shreds, wadded it into a ball and tossed it in the waste basket. "God spare me Drama Queens!"

"In my defense, I have to tell you what happened at Mother's on Tuesday." I recounted my nightmare, how my shouting had awakened her and the anxiety it had caused me. Clive stared out the window as if looking for something on the river. When I finished, he turned to me and smiled benignly.

"Don't worry," he said. "When I go, everything will be spelled out," punctuating it with his signature shrug.

"When I go! When I go! What's that supposed to mean, Clive? If that's your idea of comforting me, please try again."

"Will you relax? It's just and expression. Stop calling me on every little word." A sharp rap on the door put an end to our tête-à-tête. It was Ron Pullen, come to retrieve his charger and wondering if we had made supper plans. He'd been housebound all day, waiting on cable repair and was itching to get out for a 'real meal.' I suggested *The Old Homestead*, in easy walking distance—famous for its aged steaks and popovers—and a place I hadn't been to for years. We showed up without a reservation, were told there was a 40 minute wait which we assuaged by ordering doubles at the bar. Finally seated, Clive ordered a grilled chicken breast with several sides, while Ron and I splurged on 8 ounce sirloins. When the check arrived, Clive claimed to have left his wallet at home so Ron and I split it and called it a 'housewarming and welcome to New York' gift.

Day Twelve—Thursday, May 26th, To New Orleans.

At 5:45 am, Clive declared he was 'just too tired' to drive me to JFK and insisted on giving me $20. toward the taxi fare. As we embraced, he asked if I could FedEx him an old hairpiece from which he planned to cut a swatch and use shoe-polish to dye it for his first day on the job. I said okay while shuddering to think what it would look like—Dirk Bogarde as *von Aschenbach* in "Death in Venice" leapt to mind. I repeated expressions of unconditional love and promised to call at the end of the day.

Managed an anxious sleep throughout the flight, wondering how much of the recent histrionics was real and how much was generated by Clive simply to 'get his batteries going.' If true, and given his situation, was I not capable of the same slippery stratagem? Then there was the guilt I was feeling over escaping all that negative energy in contrast to the joy I was anticipating in returning to my cherished French Quarter digs. Add in no small amount of grief over having to vacate El Mirador after 30 years. My lawyer convinced me there was little to be gained and much to lose by attempting to challenge my landlord in a Beverly Hills courtroom. Every element of the enterprise was daunting or downright scary; potentially enormous legal fees, scheduling a trial, rounding up witnesses, taking of depositions, airfares, accommodations—hopeless! Best to STFU as they say in Cyberspeak, nurse my wounds and get on with my life. To anyone who listened, I acknowledged how grateful I was that I still had my charming slave-quarter apartment, its unique patio-garden, surrounded by caring friends and neighbors. All was not doom and gloom.

I had gone to the limit in demonstrating the meaning of 'good friend' to Clive and was reasonably confident he would rise to the challenge of rebuilding his life in the big city. I sorted through a stack of mail, answered several phone messages, called Clive as promised, left a message that I'd arrived safely then collapsed on my bed and slept for 12 hours.

Day Twenty One—Saturday, June 4th

Clive called in the morning to say that when he'd gone back to work at the insurance company, he learned it would be at least two weeks before he could draw on his account and asked if he could borrow $3,000, which he promised to pay back in two installments on June 30th and July 15th. I agreed and warned it would have to wait until Monday morning, when my bank opened and I could arrange an electronic transfer.

Over the next week and a half, we exchanged numerous phone calls and emails, commiserating over the 'two steps forward, one step back' pattern our lives seemed to have taken. He expressed delight over the new refrigerator, microwave and custom-cut wooden blinds he'd purchased with my loan.

On the 14th, I responded to a message and phoned Clive around midnight for a long phone conversation in which we again exchanged grumblings about our situations—me for having to settle for a miserly buy-out for resigning my El Mirador lease after 3 decades, he for being overwhelmed by credit-card and tax debt. A slight slurring hinted he was probably under the influence of 'the Russians.' I repeated one of my favorite platitudes, that 'we had nowhere to go but up,' which seemed to further annoy him.

Day Thirty Four—Friday, June 17th

Email: 2005/06/17 Fri PM—06:32:06 EDT
From: crew247@aol.com
To: fablano934@juno.com
Subject: Re: this is not a test…and who is YOUR top greatest American out of 25 ever? have you seen the aol list? crw"

I attended a late movie and didn't read this peculiar email until 1:00 am. Clive neglected to include a link to the AOL 'Greatest Americans' list and the one hour time difference made it too late to call for clarification. I was driving to Long Beach, MS the next morning, to spend the weekend installing window treatments at a friend's home and assumed Clive and I would catch up on Monday or Tuesday, after I returned to New Orleans. He had my cell phone number and wouldn't hesitate to call if it was anything urgent.

Day Thirty Eight—Tuesday, June 21st New Orleans

5:45 am—The jangling phone at bedside jolted me awake. In my muzzy state, I figured it must be a taxi driver informing me he was outside, waiting to take me to the airport. Then it hit me; I wasn't flying anywhere that day or anytime soon.

MALE VOICE: Bob? Is that you?
ME: Yes, it's C. Robert. Who is this?
MALE VOICE: It's Bret. From Malibu. Here, let me put Doe on. She has something to tell you.
In that instant, I know something was terribly wrong for it had to be 3:45 am in California.
DOE: C. It's about Clive.
ME: What are you saying? What about him?
DOE: He took his life.
ME: Oh my God! What do you mean—took his life? How? Where? When?
DOE: At his place in the Village. Sometime over the weekend. They found him yesterday.
ME: Oh, no, no, no. I can't believe this. It can't be true!
DOE: Bret and I are on our way to LAX. Delta thinks they can get us on their 7:00 am flight.
ME: "Oh, my God! Oh, my God, Doe! Tell me what to do. I'll do anything you ask. Just tell me what to do!"
DOE: Nothing you can do for now. We'll call you when we get to New York."

I leapt from the bed and wailed so loud, my cat retreated to his hiding place beneath it. I screamed and cried and danced macabre around my apartment. "Clive, how could you do this? To me? To everyone who loves you so? You are one of the most talented, gifted and intelligent men I have ever known. Why would you do such a terrible thing?"

After wailing like a Greek tragedienne for some minutes, at a volume that scared my upstairs neighbor into phoning me for an explanation, I decided to call Joe, my lawyer friend. My pain was excruciating and I needed to share it with someone who knew something of the situation. When I sobbed out the news, Joe became very quiet and told me it was important to 'go with your grief.' He asked me if I had any indication of how depressed Clive must have been. My answer was a qualified 'yes and no.' Clive had brushed over the subject of suicide a couple of times during our trip, but made it seem like he was 'spit-balling' ideas for one of Tom Tryon's short stories he was rewriting.

While I was on with Joe, *Call Waiting* clicked. It was Doe to say she realized she'd forgotten to give me her cell phone number, which she rattled off and immediately hung up as the final boarding call for her flight was being announced.

I spent the rest of the day mostly on the phone—booking a flight—finding a cat-sitter, alerting friends and family. A dear friend advanced $500. toward the trip. Another kindly couple made it possible for me to stay at their co-op in the Village on Jane Street, around the corner from Horatio Street. Throughout the day of frantic arrangements, my mind was a maelstrom of morbid questions: How had Clive done it? Where had he done it? Who found him? Was his body mutilated? He couldn't have used a gun, since he didn't own one. Then again, maybe he'd bought one as 'big city protection' but like he'd once said, the results would be too ghastly to contemplate. Maybe he'd jumped from a rooftop? No, that too would make for an unspeakable mess. Clive's concern for appearances would have ruled out jumping.

I concluded, incorrectly as it turned out, he must have laid hands on enough pills as he once conjectured. Why hadn't I thought to ask

Doe? Then again, maybe she was yet to be informed? And finally, what conceivable comfort could be taken if I had asked her?

Then it was on to the fear that I would be asked to identify him. God, I hoped not. Subject to fainting at the sight of blood, how could I look at Clive's lifeless body and remain standing? A phone call would distract me briefly while I explained what had happened, then I was back to thrashing myself: Writhing in guilt for feeling more victim than sympathizer. By early afternoon, uncontrollable waves of self pity had fermented into a nasty brew of grief and fury, inconsolable sadness and revulsion at his selfish act. Plus the shame for ignoring the hints and finally, disappointment at his lack of courage for not toughing it out. "For Christ's sake, Clive! If it was only about money, you could have talked it over with me, with other friends—your relatives—negotiated a settlement with the banks on the credit-card debts and started over with a clean slate." Wracked with a tsunami of emotions, I didn't sleep worth a damn that night.

Day Thirty Nine—Wednesday, June 22nd—NYC

Met Doe and Bret at the coffee shop in the Athena Plaza Hotel on East 34th Street and struggled to be stalwart through copious tears. Doe appeared remarkably calm and centered. She explained that NYPD had sealed Clive's apartment—which was standard procedure after a presumed suicide. The authorities concluded Clive's cadaver was too grotesque for viewing and Doe, shortly before my arrival, had been forced to identify him from the coroner's photos. She led me to a quiet corner of the coffee shop and read the Police report of the suicide method: 'Asphyxiation from plastic bag over head with plastic tube from *helium tank*—the kind used to inflate party balloons.' (Nano-second recall of Clive describing the balloons at Tom's memorial). This detail, combined with the owner's report of seeing empty vodka and pill bottles, confirmed how determined Clive must have been. We spent the afternoon going from Police Station to lawyer's offices to a meeting with the building owners.

In the late afternoon, Clive's two brothers and sisters-in-law arrived from Toronto. We gathered for supper at a noisy sports

149

bar/steak house on Park Avenue. After a second cocktail, one of the wives said, "We had no idea. Clive was always the star in the family." The other wife mused, "To us he led a movie-star's life." The oldest brother, obviously in his cups, began to weep. "This was all Mom's fault. Clive never wanted to be a star. She made all of us be his back-ups. I hated her for it then and I always will." His slurred denunciation set the hallmark for the evening's grief and awkwardness and brought everyone to exchange a swift and merciful 'good night.'

When I collapsed on the bed at Jane Street, I had the distinct sense that Clive's cremation had taken place at 8:30 or 9:00 pm and he was released at last. This small comfort didn't last long.

Day Forty—Thursday, June 23rd

At 3:15 I was awakened by a dream in which Clive appeared to be deeply troubled. "It's nothing like I thought it would be," he cried out. "I'm hurting all over and there doesn't seem to be any way of going back."

'Was this how it's going to be?' I asked him. 'Whenever you feel the need to communicate, you'll appear in my dreams?' I woke up before he answered. Pried myself from bed and spent the day taxiing all over Manhattan with Doe and Bret; Mid-town to the Funeral Parlor and Lawyer's Office, Downtown to City Hall and the Police Evidence vaults. We learned of a hand-written note the Police were holding for the time being, hoping it was Clive's will and might give us some indication as to how he intended to dispense his treasures. We were advised (incorrectly as it turned out) that once the Coroner released his death certificate, the Police would unseal the apartment and warned that the stench would be awful. While I taxied uptown to attend an unrelated meeting at the Time-Warner Building, Doe spoke with Clive's bosses at the insurance company. Seems he had showed up only one day over the previous two weeks—telling his bosses that he was having heart problems, simultaneously reassuring all of us that he was hard at work. Doe added, "Clive's finances look to be much, much worse than he indicated to me or anyone."

At 2:00 pm a Mass was said at St. Patrick's Cathedral. June the former roommate, one brother and sister-in-law and a pair of cast members from "A Chorus Line" attended. Later that day, I managed to lose a $100. bill climbing from a taxi while talking on my cell, having finally tracked down Jennifer Havilland to alert her of the dreadful news. Jennifer screamed so loud, it made us both cry. She immediately drove Clive's Rover into the city and generously agreed to adopt Maggie and Georgie until permanent homes could be found for them.

Day Forty one—Friday, June 24th—NYC to New Orleans.

At the conclusion of a tense, sad, exhausting, frustrating, angry-making 2 ½ days, trying to get access to Clive's apartment, handle the legal issues and steady his family while dealing with my own anguish and demons, Jennifer drove me to JFK for a 1:00 pm departure. Feeling overwhelmed by all the issues confronting me to end cycle in West Hollywood, I wondered if I was up to the challenge. Interest on my credit cards continued to accumulate at a staggering rate, with strident reminders in the daily mail. Topping it all, I learned from my New Orleans answering machine that the latest movie design prospect had evaporated for lack of financing.

"Maybe Clive had the right idea after all," I wondered to Jennifer.

"Funny, I was just thinking the same thing," she replied.

"Could I—would I consider following him?" I continued, transfixed by the logjam of traffic ahead of us. "I have several doctor friends, but what ruse could I employ to pry the pills from them? I have the reputation for being Mr. Sunny Disposition—always the hale-fellow-well-met. Everyone would become immediately suspicious if I started asking for sleeping pills. And what about Charlie, my cat? Who'd take care of him? And my unfinished novels and screenplays and my passion to create a Last Hurrah stage show in Hawaii and New Orleans? Could I ditch all that for the unlikely promise of leaving my responsibilities behind and meeting up with Clive?"

"Only you can answer that one," Jennifer shrugged, Clive-like.

"Right, which brings me to a swift conclusion: If suicide requires great courage—and surely it must—no matter its aberrant motivations—I don't have it. Never did—never could. Must have been left out of my gene pool."

"I only hope it was left out of mine," Jennifer whispered.

As we pulled up to the departures curb, I hugged and thanked her. Assured her we'd be talking soon, pulled my suitcase from the Rover and waved goodbye.

Waiting to board Jet Blue, I realized I'd be revisiting Clive's suicide and everything that preceded it, for the rest of my life.

Coda

In late July, we received word that the NYPD would release the seal on Clive's apartment so I flew to the city on a Sunday to join his sister and brothers and Jennifer in disposing of his possessions and dealing with the myriad intestate issues. It was a terrible time for all of us, in that we hoped to find a final word—some kind of instruction as to what Clive wished to be done—but there was nothing. A terse 'Farewell—don't attempt to revive me' note was read to us over the phone by a kindly detective as New York evidentiary law prevented its actual release. I returned to New Orleans on Thursday, again mentally and physically exhausted. Unable to sleep, I drafted a letter to Clive.

<u>Friday, July 29th—2:00 am</u>

Dear Clive,

What a fucking waste! You have savaged my emotions with this selfish act. Was it fear of turning 60? Worry over losing your looks? Afraid of being alone? Was it all about money? Your failed real estate investments? You were forever complaining about being forced to unload your properties at fire-sale prices," Yada, yada. What happened to courage? Offing yourself has put our 36 year friendship to an irreconcilable test! Where was your moral compass when you borrowed that last three grand from me, knowing full well you had no intention of paying it back? I read somewhere that Karmic debt, like real debt, accrues interest, but only the individuals involved can determine the rate. If true, there's not the slightest bit of comfort to be found in it for me.

I started to write, 'How dare you leave me behind?' when I realized I have no idea where you are nor any desire to be near you. Further, I've been forced to conclude that you never really believed me when I said I loved you—and I hate it. I despise even more, the evidence that you never really believed *anyone* who steeled themselves to make a declaration of love to you.

Last Monday, Ron Pullen spoke of hearing from two of your mutual friends, after each had consulted clairvoyants, one in New York and one in Los Angeles. Their independent reports from beyond concurred that you are deeply regretful for having taken

---

153

your own life, ask that we forgive and not be angry with you, and that nothing on the other side is as you'd hoped or anticipated.

As airy-fairy as all this sounds, it is consistent with my initial reaction on that terrible morning when Doe called to give me the news. After my upset with you waned, (briefly) I had the perception that, wherever you are, you are still in excruciating pain. Please know that makes two of us.

You'd often said you were sure you'd be meeting up with Tom and Rick one day—yet even a marginal understanding of how the meme of reincarnation works, and yours was more than marginal, would cast doubt on that possibility. Surely, Tom and Rick, each resolute and hubristic souls, have long since seized ownership of new bodies and are back among us? If so, did committing suicide leave you standing alone on some long-abandoned platform in the Pergatoryville train station?

Sarcasm aside, I beg you to send me some kind of sign so that I might have a fuller understanding of how this between lives business works, and what eschatological studies I might take to make it productive, should such a time befall me. Even remotely sentient, I'd prefer to deal with the situation actively, rather than reactively, as L. Ron Hubbard promised we'd be able to accomplish with the *State of Clear*. If, as I suspect, it's all total bullshit, with your help, maybe I could sue Scientology for a full refund—for both of us?

On Wednesday I received this panegyric email from your sister: "Spoke with my psychic yesterday who said that Clive is fine and glad to be out of this world. Doesn't have regrets and would do it again. Does regret, however, leaving us to pick up the pieces but knows that we can."

Should I take this as your final answer? Or is Ron Pullen's report the more accurate? I'll await your timely, unambiguous response.

I remain, your furious and grieving friend,

C. Robert

Recently

I've been listening to an orchestral version of Leonard Bernstein's *Candide* and reminded of my good fortune in having stumbled into a matinee performance of the original Broadway production those many years ago. This stately rendition, by the Minnesota Orchestra, reaffirms the tongue-in-cheek genius Bernstein conflated in his glorious score. What's more, though 12 years would pass before I met Clive and Tom, something about *Candide's* bumptiously elegant motifs inexplicably calls the two men to mind for me.

Perhaps it's the show's over-all subject matter? Or maybe it was our longed-for harkening to a more literate era? Or both? Candide to Cunegonde: 'We'll build our house and make our garden grow.' Cunegonde as kidnapped concubine to the Governor of Argentina: 'I've forgotten. Do I move towards you or away from you?' Governor: 'Away from me, whenever possible.' Dr. Pangloss: 'Listen to the fools. They believe what they're saying.'

Admiration for Voltaire's sardonic view of the human condition often nuanced our philosophical discourses. I recently read about the frequent and tortured revisions to Candide's book, lyrics and score that transpired over the operetta's fifty year history. Hyperbole bedamned, those painful revisions are not unlike what Clive and I exercised while striving for a kinder, gentler, more forthright ideal in our 35 year friendship.

That said, here I am, treading water, bouncing around my universe—avoiding a regular writing schedule, jumping from project to project—finding it impossible to focus on one idea for longer than 20 minutes. I spend endless hours getting my files in order, but I'm yet to tackle a revised will. In avoiding these issues, perhaps I'm subconsciously assigning blame in Clive's direction—which is utterly juvenile, of course. Still, it must be confronted if there's any hope for me.

A wave of exhaustion came over me as I wrote that last—as if being fearful of making some ghastly syntactical mistake, and the energy it consumes to avoid that possibility leaves me longing for a nap. What in the world is that all about? Surely, the most invidious form of writer's block?

I awoke early this morning, feeling fairly rested, with ginned-up enthusiasm for the day's tasks. iCharlie made his usual demands to get up and feed him, while various plot lines and character arcs roiled about my cluttered mind. After minor gardening efforts, reviewing email and playing a couple rounds of FreeCell, I commenced to write a second letter to Clive, when suddenly I was nodding and dozing.

His departure from this mortal coil left me with no real sparring partner on matters artistic or metaphysical. Friend Richard is disinclined to dig as deep as I like, Terrance lives in South Africa, jealously guarding his once removed aesthetic and Robert has relocated to a gentrified town in Mexico where trenchant discussions of any kind are considered déclassé—even bad for one's health.

I continue to feel sad, lonely and abandoned by Clive's escape. And, to further buttress his accusation that I am a High Priest of Hyperbole, a righteous indignation has subsumed my moxie, with the ferocity of barnacles encrusting a sunken lifeboat.

C. Robert Holloway—January 2013

As anyone who has been close to someone that has committed suicide knows, there is no other pain like that felt after the incident.
Peter Greene, Actor

<Clive Reginald Clerk-Wilson>

October 17, 1945—June 17, 2005